THE WRITER'S GUIDE TO CHARACTER EMOTION

The Writer's Guide to Character Emotion

Best Method to Crafting Realistic Character Expressions and Emotions

S. A. Soule

FWT

The Writer's Guide to Character Emotion (Book 1)
ISBN: 978-1530853410
ASIN: B00IQDW81W

Copyright © 2014 S.A. Soule

Cover art by SwoonWorthy Book Covers

FWT appreciates its readers, and every effort has been made to properly edit this guidebook. However, typos do get overlooked. If you find an error in the text, please send us an email so the issue can be corrected. Thank you!

Typesetting services by BOOKOW.COM

For dedicated fiction writers who yearn to take their writing skills to the next level!

Contents

INTRODUCTION

Dear Writer,

I've been writing most of my life, and even though I've studied the craft for years, I still love developing my skills as a writer, and I'm assuming since you purchased this book that you do, too.

First I thought I'd share a little about myself…I have over fifteen years of experience on all sides of the publishing business. I was a Creative Writing major in college, and I once owned an eBook publishing company where I edited over a hundred manuscripts. Then I worked as a developmental editor for another publisher, and in the last five years, I've even had the honor of editing books for a number of successful authors.

I've currently written eleven fiction novels and eight nonfiction titles, but it wasn't until 2015 that I became a bestselling author, and the road to success was a long journey. Many of my books have spent time on the 100 Kindle bestseller lists and some of my fiction has been chosen as top picks in the "Best Paranormal Romance" categories at several prominent review sites.

In this guide, I share some of the wisdom that I've gleamed from various workshops and online courses, along with the savvy advice from other bestselling novelists and professional editors with whom I've had the pleasure to work with in the publishing industry.

And this manual provides step-by-step instructions on ways to create realistic emotions, visceral responses, and body language, along with ways to deepen characterization that writers can easily and quickly apply to their own writing.

Even if you believe you've already mastered Deep POV, I challenge you to dig *deeper*. It doesn't matter if you are traditionally published, an Indie author, a self-published writer, or if you enjoy spending your weekends writing fanfiction, these tools can help anyone improve their storytelling abilities. Writers should use these tips as an arsenal of creative knowledge to include in their writer's toolbox.

This manual is not a "grammar do or don't" because honestly, mine is not the best, so please don't contact the literary police. My goal is always for writers to come away with stronger writing and editing abilities that they can utilize in their own stories and give their audience a more personal reading experience.

Happy writing and revising,

S. A. Soule

DEEP POINT-OF-VIEW

Quote: "In case you're unfamiliar, "show, don't tell" is the literary maxim that says stories should reveal through action (dialogue, scene, thoughts, and present conflict) instead of summary or a laundry list of descriptive details.

"Showing" is to reveal details by having your characters exemplify them, instead of the writer simply "telling" us those details outright. Done correctly, it's the difference between making your reader a participant in the story or delegating them a mere observer. Research papers and legal documents *tell*. Fiction *shows*." —*author, Jon Gingerich*

Deep Point-of-View (POV) is one of the best editing techniques that you can use to take your writing to the next level. This chapter will explain how you can revise filter words used in shallower sentences by transforming the narrative in much stronger and vivid ways.

Even if you believe you've already mastered showing vs. telling, I challenge you to absorb this handbook and go *deeper*. It doesn't matter if you are traditionally published, an Indie author, a self-published writer, or you enjoy spending your weekends writing fanfiction, these tools and techniques can help anyone improve their storytelling abilities.

Let's start with what many writers call: *Narrative Distance.*

A writer creates narrative distance (taking the reader out of the story or by reminding them that they're reading a book) when writers insert *filter words* into their writing. A Deeper POV (showing) is a much more direct and intimate way to describe a character's emotions, reactions, and actions. It will bring every scene in your novel instantly alive for your reader. And most importantly, it will keep you from using a weaker form of characterization.

Showing kicks writing up a notch by tightening, solidifying, and strengthening a manuscript. As a stellar side effect, many of those annoying problems with "show don't tell" will fade away like a bad memory.

What is Narrative Distance?

This means that the reader has been distanced, or in some cases, jolted out of the story by author intrusion. The more filter words a writer uses, the more distance they put between the reader and the story, and the less involved the reader will feel about what's happening.

Please study this example, where each sentence is *telling…*

SHALLOW:

Shawn noticed that the sky looked dark, and he felt a chill. He was scared and he wanted to go home. When he saw the shadows moving and heard a strange howling, he started to run very fast on the path.

The first scene is inert. It's too sluggish, right?

Here is a revision, where same information is *shown*...

DEEP POV:

The sky darkened and Shawn rubbed his arms against the sudden chill. His pulsed jumped. *I can't wait to get home!* The shadows shifted and the eerie howl of a wolf cut through the air. He spotted the porch lights glowing on the house and he sprinted along the path.

In the second version the reader has all the same information—dark sky, the feeling of coldness, the fear, seeing shadows, hearing the howls, introspection, and that he started running—but the revised example is vividly alive because the reader has been given something to clearly visualize rather than reading a bland report.

Personally, I'm a character-driven writer, so I *love* being inside my character's head. I want to experience their journey firsthand.

But writers often create a narrative distance when they consciously or unconsciously insert filter words into the narrative. This issue is also known as author intrusion. In my early drafts, I use a lot of filter words too, but I try to weed them out completely before my final draft. Once you start noticing them, they are easy to spot, and it becomes easier to stay in Deep POV by revising your narrative.

Deeper POV is vital to good storytelling.

This method immerses the reader so deeply in the character's skin that any external narrator simply disappears. That is, the scene is not only told from that character's perspective, but it exemplifies the character's thoughts, emotions and reactions. In other words, it's the ultimate way to *show*, not tell.

The number one reason that *showing* is more visual and appealing for the reader is that fiction is image focused, and *showing* usually generates a vivid image for the reader. Generally, *telling* doesn't produce a strong enough image on the reader's mind.

Please study this example, where the sentence is *telling*...

SHALLOW: Caleb felt hot in his wool coat.

That sentence isn't an image the reader can effortlessly imagine. It's an ambiguous fact.

DEEP POV: Caleb swiped a bead of sweat from his forehead and shrugged off his heavy winter coat.

The revised sentence puts a very powerful illustration in the reader's mind.

I realize that some filter words are mandatory in narrative, but not when you are describing the character's thoughts, emotions, or attitudes. Those should all be shown by using the Deep POV technique.

It's natural to include filter words in your early drafts. However, before you self-publish, send your manuscript off to literary agents, or post any of your short stories, you should always go back through your manuscript and revise as many filter words as you can.

By adding detailed descriptions of characters' emotions, thoughts, and actions, it will help the reader imagine the sights, sounds, smells, and textures of each scene, allowing you to take your writing to the next level.

Don't let filter words clog your prose—describe the emotion!

We feel emotions; however, we use expressions to *show* them. When you are furious, your face gets hot and your voice rises to a higher pitch. That is how people around you know that you are enraged.

You don't tell them: "Watch it. I am so mad!" No, you display it through actions, gestures, and body language. That's how real people behave.

Narrative distance also puts extra words in your sentences, which aren't needed. So, try to cut out all of the *telling* that states emotions such as: *love, hate, joy, grief, sorrow, sympathy, trepidation, fear, anger, irritation, hope, etc.* They can creep into your writing and weigh down your prose.

Over the course of this manual, I provide tons of examples from my own published novels and short stories to help you understand how to incorporate this amazing technique. Hopefully, they should spark your own creative muse and give you clever ideas on how to rewrite your shallow scenes.

Disclaimer: There are many, many ways to write in Deep POV. While this guide is only my personal opinion on this topic, it is not meant as a rule or a strict requirement. Remember, with any guides on fiction writing, trust your own instincts. Focus on the story and keep asking yourself what will make it better. As long as you do that, you pretty much can't go wrong.

So please take all of these suggestions to heart, and *only* make the changes that you feel will best suit your writing style and story.

SHALLOW WRITING

Quote: "Rather than report on emotions (i.e., he was angry, he was scared) *show* them. Yes, it's the old show don't tell. But it's true. Deep POV is the ultimate in showing. Use action, thought, and perception to show emotion and feelings. When you're annoyed, it colors your whole perception of the world. Everyone on the damn road is too damn slow and every traffic light is out to get you. Show that." —*author and editor, Ann Laurel Kopchik*

Deep POV is getting your reader so deeply submerged within the head of your characters that they experience—*really experience*—what the character is feeling. One way to stay in close-and-personal (*show*, don't *tell*) is to do this: try to reduce as many filtering references as you can from your writing.

Instead, simply *show* us what the main character *felt* and *saw* and *heard* and *decided*, without using any filter words.

If a writer overuses filtering words that clutter up each sentence and remove the reader from the experience the character is undergoing or feeling, it creates narrative distance. Anything that describes the narrator's thought or mode of perception is considered "telling" the reader. If you can revise those sentences as much as possible, the POV will feel deeper and your prose will be greatly enhanced.

Also, if a critique partner or beta reader comments on something that confused them over the emotional reaction of one of your characters, check to make sure the stimulus cause is obvious to the reader through Deep POV. I advise to always try to include some type of an emotional response and a physical reaction to intensify the moment of any scene. This helps to *show* the character's response to what is happening by using the Deep POV method.

***

To really help you understand what Deep POV is and why it will turn your novel into an unputdownable read, I have compiled examples from my own published novels.

This excerpt was taken from my book, SHATTERED SILENCE, to offer an example of how to use this wonderful technique.

The first example is what I call shallow writing and crammed with filter words. (The filter words are underlined.)

Please compare the two illustrations below...

SHALLOW:

I could <u>feel</u> my head throbbing, which <u>made</u> me reluctant to open my eyes. I <u>could tell</u> that my vision was blurry. I took deep breaths because I <u>felt</u> dizzy and I <u>knew</u> I wasn't strong enough to raise my head. I leaned on one elbow. My tongue felt like it was glued to the roof of my mouth.

A door opened, and I saw a tall woman, with short red hair, wearing dark blue scrubs and clogs. She was tough looking like a man, I thought.

"You're awake. I'm Nurse Gwen. Let me fetch the doctor." She turned around and closed the door, then locked it.

Collapsing on the thin mattress, I looked around at my foreign surroundings. I noticed stark white walls, a metal-framed bed, and a nightstand. There was a solitary window with security wiring. I heard a loudspeaker call out codes and someone yelled. I saw a fluorescent light near the ceiling. I could smell bleach from the bedding and the antiseptic scent made me feel nausea.

I have no memory of how I'd gotten here, I thought.

There were no shadows on the walls. But eventually I knew they'd come for me. I felt like I had no protection here. I felt weak and scared.

I pulled off the sheets, and swung my legs over the bed. I was dressed in a hospital gown that felt scratchy and I had a bandage wrapped around my right wrist. I noticed that I had scrapes and bruises on my arms and legs. I could see a puncture wound on my arm where someone inserted a needle.

I decided to raise one hand to touch the gauze at my temple and noticed a white band on my left wrist: *Valley Grove Psychiatric Hospital: Trudell, Shiloh*

I <u>knew</u> then that I was in the hospital.

Now this second version is written in Deep POV, but it does contain one or two filter words for better flow. *Here's a revised version that reveals (shows), instead of tells...*

DEEP POV:

My head throbbed and I was reluctant to open my eyes. My vision blurry. I took deep breaths until the waves of dizziness lessened and I was strong enough to raise my head. I leaned on one elbow. My tongue felt glued to the roof of my mouth.

A door opened, admitting a tall lady—at least six feet—with short fiery-red hair, wearing dark blue scrubs and clogs. She looked tough and very butch. Bet nobody messed with her.

"You're awake. I'm Nurse Gwen. Let me fetch the doctor." She whipped around and closed the door. Locked it.

Collapsing on the thin mattress, I surveyed my foreign surroundings. Stark white walls, a metal-framed bed, and a nightstand. Solitary window with security wiring. Somewhere a loudspeaker called out codes and someone howled loudly. Fluorescent light glared down from the ceiling. Whiffs of bleach wafted from the bedding and the antiseptic scent gave me nausea.

I had no memory of how I'd gotten here.

No shadows danced on the walls. But eventually they'd come for me. I had no protection here. I was weak. Defenseless. Vulnerable.

I yanked off the crisp sheets, and swung my legs over the cold metal bed. Someone had dressed me in a scratchy hospital gown and wrapped my right wrist in an elastic Ace bandage. I had scrapes and bruises on my arms and legs. My forearm had a puncture wound where someone had inserted a needle. I raised one hand to touch the gauze at my temple and gasped at the band on my left wrist that read: *Valley Grove Psychiatric Hospital: Trudell, Shiloh*

Oh, no! I was in the nut house!

***

When *telling*, the writer is making a statement. Readers are being told (telling) what to believe by the writer, rather than the readers discovering things for themselves.

Remember that these are just "guidelines" to help improve your skills as a writer. Occasionally breaking the 'rules' is what a story calls for. But don't do it too often. By trying to create meaningful, descriptive prose, it will naturally move the story forward and convey a richer experience for your reader. Don't weigh it down with filter words.

I'm assuming that since you purchased this handbook, it's because you want to improve your writing skills. If you use the Deep POV technique, I promise that you'll notice an amazing difference in your writing. And I bet your readers will, too!

SHOWING

Quote: "Like many other techniques, Deep POV cannot be perfected overnight. At first, a keen eye and a conscious mind must work together to keep the work from slipping back into typical shallow POV techniques. However, writing in Deep POV continuously will help the technique become a natural part of your writing style." —*Kristen Kieffer, writer and blogger*

So now you've written a remarkable story, and had your manuscript ruthlessly edited by your critique partners and read by your insightful beta readers...but is it ready to be self-published or submitted to literary agents yet?

First, ask yourself:

What are some of the generally overlooked mistakes writers make that send red flags to agents and publishers that their work isn't polished?

What common mistakes do many self-published writers make that instantly turn readers off?

Even an experienced writer like myself always needs to triple-check my work before sending it out into the world. I continuously need to go back and revise all those annoying filter words. *Showing* engages the reader in ways *telling* (shallow writing) often can't do as successfully.

For example, readers need details. They need to know the thoughts, feelings, and reactions to every occurrence. Instead of *telling* readers what those reactions and actions are, I would just let the reader figure it out for themselves. Readers need to smell the flowers, taste the apple, experience the fear, and feel the silky fabric of a dress. Anything less than that cheats the reader from deeply experiencing our fictional world.

Examine these two examples. The first is written in Shallow POV and the second is revised into a much Deeper POV and it includes a few of the five senses, and even "voice" to bring the scene to life. Please carefully compare these examples...

SHALLOW:

Simone saw the zombie shamble through the doorway. It had green drool coming from its mouth and the sight made Simone feel sick. The bad smell coming from the zombie's body caused her to cover her mouth and nose. She looked around for a weapon. She didn't notice anything handy, and realized that she was about to be attacked. She swallowed a frustrated scream.

DEEP POV:

The zombie shambled into the room. Toxic green saliva dripped from its mouth and she backed up. A sickly putrid stench of decay rose from the drooling brain-muncher. Simone almost gagged, pinching her nose with one hand. Her gaze quickly scanned the space. No guns. No real weapons.

This is not good! Her heart rate tripled. She grabbed a baseball bat from the closet and faced the walking dead. *Game on.*

***

When a writer doesn't use Deep POV, it is called "telling." Most new writers use shallow writing, because they are not applying the Deep POV method.

A few common filter words include: *considered, regarded, wondered, saw, heard, hoped, realized, smelled, watched, touched, felt,* and *decided.*

These types of weak words are often used when the author wants to inform the reader of the character's reactions or emotions, rather than describing them directly. "Telling" is a method of expressing facts to the reader, but it is usually the *incorrect* way. In this handbook, I offer some practical ways to identify filter words and phrases.

When I was writing my new adult novel, SMASH INTO YOU, I used a lot of shallow writing and filter words in the first few drafts, and then I went back and deepened the POV to *show.*

Please study this example...

EXAMPLE (early draft): Everywhere I looked, I saw older, tall buildings.

It conveys the info about the setting in a dull and un-visual way, and it worked while I was stilling in the drafting stage.

Here is the revision, where the same information is *shown*...

EXAMPLE (final draft): All around me stood lofty buildings constructed of brick and stone, crowned by shingled rooftops and spires, tradition and pride oozing from every cornerstone.

Did you grasp the difference?

My point is, tell all you want in early drafts of a story. Then go back and revise with a deeper POV. For instance, if a writer states that a character is grief-stricken it is shallow writing.

SHALLOW: Megan was distraught over her husband's death.

That first example is *telling* the reader in a shallow way that Megan is grieving, which is fine. However, once the revision work starts, then that same statement should be revised into *showing*.

Please study this revised example...

EXAMPLE: Her heart seemed to spiral into a deep abyss followed by a hollow ache swelling inside her chest. The physical pain was suddenly too much to endure.

Which example had more impact?

The second example provides a deeper POV and a better visual, and it's for reasons of dramatic impact that *showing* is commonly encouraged over *telling*. When a writer does use "telling," it is to keep the pace of the story moving forward.

***

Here is an excerpt taken from my novel, LOST IN STARLIGHT that shows how using Deep POV correctly will enhance any scene.

DEEP POV:

Hayden glances in my direction and his extraordinary eyes lock onto mine. An unfamiliar thrill shoots through my veins. Even from a short distance, the boy looks mouthwatering good. His eyes harden into chips of ice.

Although I'm obviously busted, I can't look away. For a second, his gaze flares into the hottest flame. As though ignited by kerosene, my body temperature rises. There's a wariness lingering in his expression that I don't understand. Finally, I tear my gaze away and a fierce spark of panic hits hard.

Is my hair tangled? My pencil skirt unzipped? Lip gloss on my teeth?

Pulling a quick ninja hair check, I look out the nearby window, surreptitiously using the reflection to ensure that my flyaway hair looks tame. I sweep a hand around my waist to check my zipper and run my tongue over my teeth. All good. I grip the hem of my black tee under my leather jacket, the silver studded leather cuff on my wrist digging into my stomach, and yank it down. Much better.

Possibly embarrassing situation averted.

***

Did you grasp how I stay in Deep POV throughout that scene? Great!

Here is an excerpt written in Deep POV from the novel, "The Traveler" by John Katzenbach:

She felt suddenly overcome by heat, as if one of the spotlights had singled her out, covering her with a solid beam of intense brightness. She gulped a great breath of air, then another, fighting a dizzying sensation. She remembered the moment years earlier when she'd realized that she was shot, that the warmth she felt was the lifeblood flowing from her, and she fought with the same intensity to prevent her eyes from rolling back, as if giving into the blackness of unconsciousness would be as fatal now as it would have been then.

***

Within that excerpt, the author does use a filter word or two, but he still manages to stay close-and-personal with a tight POV.

Want to know how to become a powerhouse of a writer?

Simply, start using a Deeper POV. The right way to "show" is by revealing information through action, dialogue, and the five senses. Learn to be ruthless and revise any shallow sentences.

TELLING

Quote: "Telling speeds up the pace when we don't want to add another ten paragraphs...we can "tell" when we need to include a number of vital, yet minor events that aren't particularly dramatic. The purpose of those scenes is to bring readers up to the present without interfering with the pace...Or if our story moves along, and we introduce an unfamiliar element to readers, we interject a one or two sentence explanations and move on." —*author, Cecil Murphey*

While there are a lot of writing blogs and professional editors that offer advice on showing vs. telling, most of them don't explain when to "tell" and *not* show in writing. So I've listed a few in this chapter...

The contrasts of showing vs. telling:

Telling is when a writer provides the reader with direct facts, or explains a situation, or offers important information in relation to the storyline in a straightforward manner. This approach is considered passive writing that summarizes events that aren't really significant to the plot, but they are necessary to fill in plot holes or get the info across quickly to keep the story moving forward.

In general, telling requires using fewer words to convey details, but those sentences should still be written with "voice." (I go into much more detail about character "voice" and a writer's narrative style in book two, "The Writer's Guide to Deep POV," if you're interested on learning more about those topics.)

Also, *telling* is kind of an old-fashioned way of storytelling. Although, recently I read three traditionally published authors that still do way too much telling with info-dumps that made me put the book down while yawning, and then pick up a different novel...

Showing is sensationalizing and digging deeper. It vividly conveys more of a visual for the reader through visceral, impactful, and evocative writing that allows them to effortlessly imagine the story-world, as well as the characters you've created. A deeper POV is considered active writing, but it is typically more wordy and descriptive.

Also, (showing) Deep POV relates to almost every sentence in a story, and can be conveyed through the author's use of language, through the syntax and word choices.

When writing in Deeper POV, everything that happens in a scene is processed in a unique way by that POV character, so even the narrative (telling) must have "voice."

I know some of you are asking: So when is it okay to just *tell* the reader something?

While there are many different methods to *showing* in writing, there are just as many reasons to *tell* when needed.

Showing vs. telling is all about balance.

To me personally, *showing* is used when a writer wants a Deeper POV, and *telling* is needed when the reader requires certain information pertaining to the timeline or plot. *Telling* is for informing the reader in a passive way, like giving them the bare bones.

For instance, whenever the writer gives the reader information in a direct manner, it is considered telling. But it can also make the reader feel somewhat removed from the immediate experience of the moment.

In spite of that, if a writer showed *everything*, then it would cause a lot of overwriting and major pacing issues within the manuscript. Some parts of a story are so inconsequential that writers might want the reader to known a fact or small detail, without going into too much description. If the details or facts are only supplemental to the scene, then it's perfectly okay to just tell the reader. Because if a writer were to *show* every single thing, then the reader would consider the scene padded.

And there's nothing wrong with *telling* in early drafts of a manuscript. Most writers do it because the important thing is to get the story written, and then go back and fill in any plot holes. Using Deep POV comes later, after five or six drafts are finished, when it's time to *dig deeper* in some scenes and revise the characterization. There is no need to stop writing the first or second draft to include carefully detailed descriptions or a Deeper POV. That can wait.

There are no hard-and-fast rules when it comes to showing vs. telling, but a few instances where it would better to "tell" would be these:

1) To convey the passing of time

2) When a character travels from one location to another

3) When backstory is essential to a scene

4) When world-building is necessary

TIME

Let's discuss the first reason. When a writer wants to convey the passage of time to the reader, it is much quicker to just state that a few days have passed or even months. However, a writer should still *show* it through "voice."

In my novel, LOST IN STARLIGHT, I wanted to skip the duller parts of the story whenever the main character was in school, so I summarized when required.

Let's take a look at one example…

EXAMPLE: My afternoon classes zoom by like movie trailers. And then the theater goes dark right before the film starts, and mercifully the last bell rings. I'm finally free.

Did you grasp how I showed the passing of time?

The short paragraph lets the reader know that school has ended without a long info-dump of shallower writing.

Here's another example...

EXAMPLE: Miss Rogers had kept Charlene after school, giving the entire class a lengthy and dull lecture in French. When class finally ended, Charlene rushed out of the heavy doors, buttoning her strawberry-colored Agnes B. trench coat as she went outside.

Now if the paragraph above had gone into more detail about the teacher's longwinded speech, then the passage would've become a dull lecture for the reader as well.

Another example is in Stephenie Meyer's book, NEW MOON, where she states the passage of time by simply having chapters listed with the name of the month, but no other text or explanation is given. The reader infers that (spoiler alert!) months have passed since Edward left and how long poor Bella has been wallowing in her heartache.

TRAVEL

Now onto the second reason why a writer should tell instead of show. To speed things up in a scene, it might be better to just state that character got from point A to point B without being too descriptive.

Readers don't need specifics regarding a long drive, or a plane ride, or even exactly how a character managed to get from one place to another. In other words, if nothing vital to the plot happens, then just tell the reader.

In my novel, IMMORTAL ECLIPSE, the character went from New York to California, but I didn't bother with boring details regarding the drive to the airport or about checking in at the airport, itself.

Let's take a look these examples...

EXAMPLE: It takes two trips to haul my luggage downstairs, which leaves me panting. Talk about a workout. I hail a cab for the airport and three hours later, I'm boarding the plane.

Please carefully study this next example...

EXAMPLE: After departing Matthew Rosenberg's office, I'm too jet-lagged to drive the two hours into Carmel, so I check in to the San Francisco Hyatt overnight and play tourist. I roam Fisherman's Wharf, snapping pictures of the neighborhood, and later I devour a scrumptious dinner at a Pier 39 waterfront cafe before falling into bed for the night.

Sunday morning I awake to a thick fog shrouding the city and order room service. I have scrambled eggs and a mocha for breakfast before starting the two-hour journey to Carmel.

Did you grasp how I told the reader that a day has passed? I needed to include those short paragraphs in the novel to fix a plot hole in my timeline.

The next paragraph taken from one of my novels basically states that the character drove from one location (school) to another (graveyard) without going into too much detail because nothing eventful happened plotwise.

Please carefully study this example...

EXAMPLE: But instead of going to study hall as I was instructed, I speed-walk to the school parking lot. Twenty minutes later, I park my VW Jetta near the arched entrance of Shadowland Memorial Cemetery.

Quick and to the point!

These examples should give writers a few clever ideas on other ways to convey that a character traveled from place to another without a long info-dump.

BACKSTORY

There's really only one way to let the reader get a *glimpse* of a character's past, and that's by telling them.

Now a writer could reveal it in a flashback, but that's a topic for another book. Or they could use common tropes like a diary, or even through dialogue, but it often comes across akin to, "As you know, Bob..." which can be annoying to readers.

Writers should disclose a character's backstory through "voice," action, and dialogue. And most importantly, it should just be sprinkled throughout the narrative—and *never* dumped.

In my novel, BEAUTIFULLY BROKEN (free to read and download for a limited time), the reader needed some background info about the main character's dysfunctional family.

THE WRITER'S GUIDE TO CHARACTER EMOTION

Please carefully study this example…

EXAMPLE: After a heartbeat, I relaxed my shoulders and stared at the small trunk as though it contained all the hidden mysteries of the Underworld. I never had a chance to question Aunt Lauren about the trunk after she'd given it to me. To ask about either the books or the prophecy. After that, she wasn't allowed in our house. No one would explain why. But I'd heard. Statements hurled out like spears. Hurtful words that could never be taken back once spoken. A family divided by silence.

It majorly sucked because my family used to be close. Since my tenth birthday, Aunt Lauren and my grandparents, Grandma Naomi and Grandpa Samuel, didn't come around as much. I missed them. Their absence caused me to feel even more alone in the world.

Could you perceive how I used "voice" to keep it from becoming too info-dumpy?

Backstory when done well can often deepen characterization and tie into the story's theme.

Please carefully study this next example…

EXAMPLE: My ancestors had escaped the violent witch-hunts in England and France by coming to America in the middle of the 17ᵗʰ century. Rumor had it that they had brought magick with them to Ravenwood. Started over here. Away from persecution and prying eyes. They had tapped into the arcane power confined within nature and prospered. And I *had* somehow opened the blinds covering my bedroom window this morning. By my own sheer force of will…or by magick? It was still hard for me to believe.

Did you notice how the backstory unfolds with some interesting tension?

To avoid backstory becoming an info-dump, a writer should never include those dreaded chunks of backstory that are spewed onto to the page in one long block of text that can cause the plot to come to a skidding halt.

WORLD-BUILDING

Every story needs a solid and vivid fictional world for the reader to envision.

In certain genres such as, fantasy, historical, or science fiction, world-building is essential to the plot and for readers to understand and visualize the story-world. (I dig deeper into the topic of world-building in another guidebook, "The Writer's Guide To Vivid Settings and Characters" if you're interested in learning more about description.)

These types of stories necessitate detailed settings and descriptions of clothing, modes of transportation, food, housing, etc. But a writer should always describe these types of specifics through sensory details even when doing an info-dump. In a way, world-building is like the backstory of the story. (I am not going to go into too much detail in this chapter about world-building or when to *tell* because I plan to write another book in this "Deep POV" series that will expand on this topic.)

As the narrative progresses, writers should introduce only the elements relevant to the scene, the theme, the characters, and the plot. Whenever a writer is describing the setting, they should include action and "voice" and sensory details.

Please carefully study this next example…

EXAMPLE: As I walk out of the quiet, air-conditioned comfort of the bookstore, I'm immediately hit by a blast of hot air from the street. I unzip my windbreaker and tie the sleeves around my waist.

Tall buildings with their concrete heads in the clouds crowd the business district, and the grumble of trucks and cars passing by resemble a congested river of vehicles rushing toward an unknown destination.

I maneuver around a hot dog vendor, wiping his sweaty brow, but bump into office-workers on their lunch break. Smartly dressed men and women hurrying in the direction of a cafe further down the street. The mixture of onion, garlic, pepper, and other spices create a potent combination that tingles my nose.

Holding my breath for a moment, I hurry past the Italian restaurant and cross the street. I've always wondered how the people working inside can stand the odor of garlic. *Ugh.*

At the next corner, I pause, shifting my weight from foot-to-foot while I wait for the signal to blink "walk" before I cross the busy street. The light changes to green and I step off the curb —right into the path of a big, black SUV. My body bounces on the hood, pain ripping through my limbs. Shards of glass from the windshield slash into my skull and torso.

When I woke up hours later in the hospital, my head is bandaged and I'm sporting a white plaster cast on my left leg. The sterile, white room reeks of disinfectant and strong soap.

Could you vividly imagine the setting? Visualize the busy city streets? Smell the aroma of spices?

Whenever *telling*, try to avoid doing an info-dump (when information is being dumped in blocks of text onto the page without a break with action or dialogue) is a type of exposition that is particularly wordy and often dull. Although, some info-dumping can be done in a way that is interesting and even compelling, most exposition is noticeably intrusive. It usually makes a reader want to skim past the pages of wordy descriptions to get back to the action.

Another thing that writers should watch out for is any *showing* that becomes "Purple Prose." That's when the writing is so ostentatious, flowery, and overwritten that it breaks the story's flow and draws unnecessary attention to itself.

In fact, I used to be the queen of "purple prose" when I was a young writer. And I think I'm still guilty of it on occasion. But then again, I do enjoy reading some purple prose if the writer is skilled enough to pull it off.

As you revise your story, remember that Deep POV will help to lure the reader into each character's head so completely that your readers will feel as if they are experiencing everything that happens right alongside your narrator, so always try to *dig deeper.*

INFO-DUMPS

Quote: "Deep POV allows writers to do away with *he thought, he felt, he wondered, he saw,* all those phrases that unnecessarily encumber a story. At one time such phrases were necessary to let readers know we were in the character's head or seeing through his eyes. With deep POV, readers are in the character's head [almost] all the time, and so such intrusions aren't necessary." *—fiction editor, Beth Hill of "A Novel Edit"* (I had the honor of working with Beth on my novel, IMMORTAL ECLIPSE, and she's an amazing editor.)

An info-dump can be a way of "telling" a reader, instead of describing it. As you revise your novel instead of stating the emotion for the reader, resulting in long passages of exposition, try to include some action, emotion, and reaction within the scene. Make use of the five senses: hearing, sight, touch, smell, and taste. Try to include descriptive words and Deep POV to enhance everything you write. You don't have to use each sense in every scene; one or two in any given situation will transform an otherwise tedious scene into a tangible and vivid experience for your reader.

Plus, telling the reader everything the character thinks or feels is boring and not needed. Instead, try to *show* by using Deep POV, which can and will enrich your story.

Please carefully compare these examples. The filter words are underlined.

SHALLOW:

Jennifer <u>entered</u> her bedroom and frowned. She <u>smelled</u> her best friend's perfume and her husband's cologne. She <u>felt angry</u>. She <u>decided</u> that he must have been cheating on her.

DEEP POV:

Jennifer walked into her bedroom, planning to surprise her husband with a ten year anniversary gift. She stopped short and raised a trembling hand to her chest. *Oh, god. No!*

Her stomach lurched. The faint trace of her best friend's perfume lingered in the air, mingled with the musk scent of Jack's aftershave. *That lying, cheating jerk!*

***

Using Deeper POV will heighten every scene in your story and make your dialogue come to life.

This next example was taken from my novel, SHATTERED SILENCE. Again, the shallower words are underlined. Please compare these examples...

SHALLOW (before revision):

Just when I thought my night couldn't possibly get any stranger...

I felt pain hurting the scar on my forearm. It burned. I felt tremors throughout my body. The mark began to vibrate and felt feverish. I slightly screamed in pain.

My dad and my aunt Lauren, standing beside me, instantly became concerned.

Dad rubbed my back. "Honey bunch, are you okay?"

I knew I couldn't talk, but I could nod. Something bad was here. I knew it.

"Relax, Shiloh. Just breathe," Aunt Lauren said. "Do you feel sick?"

I heard the doorbell chime.

I took a step back, bumping an end table. A vase fell over onto the floor. I felt an unnerving expectancy in the room. I felt like I was being smothered.

I watched Aunt Lauren bend down to pick up the vase. I saw my mother—Darrah—cross the room to answer the door.

I was scared. I knew something bad was ringing the doorbell. I felt like screaming and telling my mother, no.

***

This revised version written in Deeper POV *shows* the different emotions that the character is experiencing in this short scene.

Deep POV (after revision):

Just when I thought my night couldn't possibly get any stranger…

Pain pulsed across the jagged scar on my forearm. My mark burned, sharp and quick, like it did whenever something dangerous was around. My chest hurt. Tremors raked my limbs. The mark on my forearm vibrated and became feverish. A short scream tore from my lips.

My dad and my aunt Lauren, standing beside me, instantly became concerned.

Dad rubbed my back. "Honey bunch, are you okay?"

I couldn't speak, only nod. Something bad was here. I knew it in my bones.

"Relax, Shiloh. Just breathe," Aunt Lauren said. "Do you feel sick?"

The doorbell chimed.

Little pig, little pig, please, let me come in…

I took a step back, bumping an end table. A vase crashed to the floor. The room brimmed with an unnerving expectancy. I felt smothered, like I was crammed into a dangerous and airless place.

Aunt Lauren bent down to pick up the shards of porcelain from the vase. My mother—Darrah—crossed the room to answer the door.

Oh, god. It was here. Now. Ringing my damn doorbell.

I wanted to scream, *No! Don't open that door!*

***

These examples should help you to revise your own story into a gripping read!

FILTER WORDS

Quote: "Filtering words are generally words that you add to a sentence when you are trying to describe something that your character is experiencing or thinking. These can be sense words like *feel, taste, see, hear,* and *smell,* or variations thereof. Writers don't necessarily have to avoid these words, but they should be aware of the effect that they have on your prose. Rather than describing a sensation outright, you are distancing your reader from the sense that you are describing." —*young adult author, Corrine Jackson*

Inner-monologue or internal exposition is one of the essential ingredients used to create a comprehensive story. But unfortunately, it's all too often one of the most misused elements in storytelling and can be weakened with too many filter words.

Since internal-monologue is slower and can be boring for the reader, find ways to bring it to life through Deep POV. Don't let your character's mental babble (long blocks of introspection) go on for pages at a time without a break by either dialogue or action.

Dialogue illustrates characterization quicker than any amount of exposition. If you disrupt the action and dialogue to include colossal chunks of description or introspection, it will remove the reader from the story.

Try to start each scene with a compelling bit of action, dialogue, and intrigue. Once the reader is "hooked," then go ahead and add in the necessary exposition. Too much introspection or shallow writing can hinder the flow of the scene and smack of author intrusion by yanking the reader out of the story. It is so much more powerful to be *shown* rather than *told* a character's thoughts, decisions, reactions, and feelings. In active scenes, interior monologue is also a powerful tool to make scenes more emotional and cause your dialogue to sparkle. Internal dialogue is a very effective technique, but one that should be used sparingly.

In almost every scene, I think it's important to stay in Deep POV. One way is to try to reduce the number of filtering references. So rather than: "he/she think or thought," or "he/she felt, he/she see or saw," or "he/she hear or heard," or "he /she noticed," or "he/she realized," or "he/she wondered," or "he/she decided," or even "he/she wished," simply describe the emotion or thought or feeling through Deep POV.

Examples of weak filter words are underlined, along with examples on how to revise your sentences into Deep POV. Please carefully compare these sentences ...

SHALLOW: I thought Tom was being a jerk.

DEEP POV: Tom was acting like a major jerkwad!

SHALLOW: Sammy felt the floor shake.

DEEP POV: The floor shook violently beneath Sammy's feet.

SHALLOW: Katie <u>realized</u> that she had forgotten her keys.

DEEP POV: *Oh, no!* Where did she leave her keys?

SHALLOW: I <u>saw</u> the cat pounce on the mouse.

DEEP POV: The cat crouched, tail swishing. Then the feline pounced on the unsuspecting mouse.

SHALLOW: Reed <u>heard</u> her mom's car pull into the driveway.

DEEP POV: Reed's ears perked up at the crunch of tires on the driveway.

SHALLOW: I <u>noticed</u> that Zander was angry.

DEEP POV: Zander's face reddened and he balled up his fist. *Ah, crud.*

SHALLOW: Sharon <u>wondered</u> if her daughter, Jill had passed her history test.

DEEP POV: Sharon frowned. *I sure hope Jill aces that test!*

SHALLOW: I <u>decided</u> to confront Zach during lunch.

DEEP POV: Instead of going to my usual table at lunch, I bypass my friends and their curious stares and storm right up to Zach.

SHALLOW: Max <u>wished</u> for a new bike more than anything for his birthday.

DEEP POV: Max put the ad for the bike in his mother's cookbook. *That should be a clear hint!*

***

I realize that writers cannot remove every occurrence of filtering, but they can revise those shallower words whenever possible. Just remember that Deep POV respects the reader's intelligence. Shallow writing (telling) presumes that your reader isn't clever enough to understand unless the writer states the emotion. But if you use the Deep POV method, it will immerse the reader into the story and induce an emotional response, which gives them a much deeper reading experience.

Another way to really use Deep POV effectively is to give each of your characters a distinctive "voice" that comes across in your narrative. Choose your words carefully, because they will reveal a lot about your character and vividly *show* their unique voice.

Please study these two examples from my published novel, IMMORTAL ECLIPSE:

SHALLOW (no voice):

I looked at the cream envelope on the kitchen table. Is it a wedding invitation? I thought. I hated being unmarried and having people give me a hard time about it. I didn't understand why being single and in my late twenties made my married friends give me odd looks. I was just independent.

DEEP POV:

My gaze rests on the cream envelope lying on the kitchen table. The one I'd first thought was a wedding invitation. Yet another nail in my unmarried-still-tragically-single coffin. Why does being single equate to being tossed in the bargain bin at Target? I'm a sophisticated and independent New Yorker, dammit!

***

Each sentence portrays the same scenario, but how the character reacts and is *shown* in the wording used to convey her thoughts and feelings is vastly different and gives the reader a Deeper POV. The first one is "telling" the reader info in a weak shallow way, but in the second version, we get a glimpse of her personality and "voice" and it is written in Deep POV.

To avoid filter words, a useful tool to help search out and eliminate repetitive or unproductive words is the FIND and RE-PLACE function in Microsoft Word. Either delete the weak word entirely or revise the sentence into actively showing. Alternatively, print the page and use a colored highlighter to single out needless words, and then re-edit the scene.

Don't let weak filter words distance your writing. Most of those words can be deleted, and by using Deep POV instead, it will give your writing greater impact. Just remember that you should always strive to *show* the emotion instead of telling the reader. The next few chapters will cover this in more detail with some great examples on how to revise your prose into a Deeper POV.

In the subsequent chapters, I have listed helpful examples on how to revise filter words.

*Note: All of the Deep POV examples in this handbook have already been used in my published books or short stories, so you'll need to come up with your unique variations.

SHALLOW: FELT

Quote: "A skill that leads straight into strong, emotive writing is Deep Point Of View. And I mean *deep*. This is often a very hard skill to conquer...Deep POV is an art, because it's putting yourself so totally into the character you [the author] basically don't appear because it's *all* the character. What also disappears in deep POV to a great extent is "tags" —the "he thought/ pondered/ wondered" that jerk readers out of the character's head, reminding them that they are not the hero or heroine— and that's what we, as writers, don't want!" *—author, Melissa James*

In my opinion, *felt / feel* is the weakest word there is to describe an emotional reaction to something. In this chapter, I will show you examples on how to eliminate the biggest "telling" offender of filter words: *felt / feel / feeling / feels* from your writing, and how to transform the sentences below into vivid sensory details by using the Deep POV method.

Writing with filter words "I felt" or "He had a feeling" or "It feels so soft" or "I feel angry" is almost never necessary in Deeper POV. Instead of saying "he/she felt" something, simply describe the emotion instead.

So I strongly encourage writers to revise as many occurrences of filter words like *felt* as they can from the manuscript before self-publishing, posting an online story, or sending any work off to a literary agent or publishing editor. Writers cannot remove them all, but any shallow writing that directly describes an emotion *can* and should be revised.

Whenever possible revise these filter words: FELT / FEEL

SHALLOW: I felt a hand slap me sharply across the face.

DEEP POV: My head snapped back from the hard slap, my cheeks stinging from the unexpected blow.

SHALLOW: I felt angry, suddenly.

DEEP POV: Flaring my nostrils, I stomped forward and got right in Missy's face.

SHALLOW: He felt queasy.

DEEP POV: His stomach lurched, his breakfast threatening to cough back up.

SHALLOW: Charles felt his cheeks go red.

DEEP POV: Charles' cheeks heated, a red stain coloring his face.

SHALLOW: He felt as though the top of his head would explode.

DEEP POV: His head pounded and his thoughts swirled.

SHALLOW: Jack feels unsteady on his feet.

DEEP POV: Jack wobbles forward, his legs unsteady.

SHALLOW: Mary felt a tightening in her stomach.

DEEP POV: Mary's stomach tightened.

SHALLOW: Scott felt his chest go tight.

DEEP POV: A deep ache snapped through him.

SHALLOW: Her heart feels as if it had just flopped over inside her ribcage.

DEEP POV: Her heart flops over inside her ribcage.

SHALLOW: She felt drowsy.

DEEP POV: Unable to stifle a yawn, she pulled up the blankets and closed her eyes.

SHALLOW: Lisa felt so disappointed and mad.

DEEP POV: Lisa's bottom lip trembled. She kicked at the ground with her sneaker. *This sucks!*

***

FELT / FEEL are filter words that will convey obvious information, while neatly inserting the dreaded narrative distance. The fact that the character *felt* whatever happens is understood by the reader without being told.

Please carefully compare these examples...

SHALLOW:

Max felt a flare of jealousy when he noticed his ex-girlfriend, Tammi with the new guy at work. Then he calmed down a little, deciding Tammi wasn't worth wasting his time.

He took a breath and pulled on his suit jacket. Then he looked over again and saw them kissing near the front counter.

Max felt so enraged that he felt his body tense up. The rage in his heart felt like it would explode. He moved closer to the office window and felt like he wanted to kill that guy.

He watched the new employee hitting on his girlfriend. Max knew Tammi belonged to him.

DEEP POV:

Max's mouth dropped open at the sight of ex-girlfriend, Tammi, flirting with the new guy at work. Heat boiled his insides. Then he relaxed his shoulders and blew out a breath.

Calm yourself, Max. She isn't worth wasting your time.

He tugged on his jacket, preparing to sell more cars today then the dirtbag chatting up his ex. But when he glanced over at them again, his chest tightened. The new guy had his tongue down Tammi's throat near the receptionist's desk. At work. In front of everybody.

Eyes narrowed and nostrils flared, he stomped closer to the office window to glare at them through the glass. Every muscle in his body tensed up.

Tammi's my girl! That new dude was gonna be nothing more than an oil stain when he was done plummeting him into the ground.

***

After reading the two different examples, could you see how *naming the emotion* and using filter words creates narrative distance?

The second example is a perfect illustration on how to describe a character's emotional state without *naming* the feeling.

In the succeeding chapters, I have listed tons of helpful examples of filter words that take you out of Deep POV. Again, all of these examples have already been used in my published books, but they should help spark your own creative muse and give you some ideas on how to modify your own wonderful stories.

SHALLOW: SEE

Quote: "Going through 100,000 words and looking at every use of "saw," "see," "seeing," and "seen" is time consuming and tedious. On the other hand, I think the search function forces writers to stop on things that we would otherwise miss in our writing. You can't gloss over something without noticing it when it's highlighted in yellow. When I'm stopped like that, I find I'm much more objective about my sentences." —*writer and blogger, Michael J. McDonagh*

"Sight" is one of the main senses that a character would use to describe something, since people depend on sight more than any of the other senses.

When a writer states that a character "saw something" or when a character describes a place (setting) or an object, use the sense of sight to vividly describe it with colors, shapes, and an emotional reaction. Be detailed, yet have fun with the description!

Now I feel that it is perfectly okay to use "watch" in a sentence if it adds to the scene. For example, *As I watch him walk away, the cold night swallows him and a dark flutter strikes my chest, like a bird smashing itself against a window.* However, if the word "watch/watched" gets overused in your manuscript, or if it is being used as a filter word, than I would revise that sentence.

Always strive to revise filter words like *see / saw / could see* in a scene, and instead just describe whatever he/she saw.

Whenever possible revise these filter words: SAW / SEE

SHALLOW: I see the moon lift overhead.

DEEP POV: The moon hung in an inky sky overhead.

SHALLOW: He saw things moving, shifting.

DEEP POV: Things were moving, shifting.

SHALLOW: He saw nothing that threatened danger.

DEEP POV: He sensed nothing that threatened danger.

SHALLOW: She saw something out a window.

DEEP POV: Moving closer to the window, she peered through the glass.

SHALLOW: He sees the blue glow of the stars, and a milky ring around the moon.

DEEP POV: Glancing upward, he stares at the blue glow of the stars, and a milky ring around the moon.

SHALLOW: Sarah saw that he was wearing a black ski mask.

DEEP POV: Sarah stumbled back when he stepped forward wearing a black ski mask.

SHALLOW: He sees her sleek body moving through the water.

DEEP POV: He admires her sleek body moving through the water.

SHALLOW: I could see glints of gold in his blond hair.

DEEP POV: Glints of gold shone in his blond hair.

Whenever possible revise these filter words: WATCH

SHALLOW: He watched the bird bobbing its head up and down.

DEEP POV: The bird was bobbing its head up and down.

SHALLOW: He watched as she walked back into the kitchen.

DEEP POV: She walked back into the kitchen, her hips swaying, and he smiled faintly to himself.

SHALLOW: I watched my father walk into the motel.

DEEP POV: I moved out of the way as my father strode into the motel.

SHALLOW: He saw Melanie put the lipstick into her purse and head out of the store.

DEEP POV: Glancing down the aisle, his eyes popped wide. Melanie slipped the lipstick into her bag, and then walked out of the store.

SHALLOW: Cary watched her car drive away and felt his heart sink in his chest.

DEEP POV: Cary stayed on the porch as she drove away, his heart sinking lower in his chest.

SHALLOW: Maggie <u>could see</u> the snowcapped mountains from the window of her hotel room.

DEEP POV: Throwing back the curtains, Maggie had a clear view of the snowcapped mountains from the window of her hotel room.

***

Effective Deep POV requires that you take your readers through the emotional experiences of your character as your character actually experiences them.

Using filter words like *watched / see / saw* only distances your reader and takes you out of Deeper POV, which is not what you want.

Again, let's use another example in order to clarify what I mean. Here's a snippet from my book, LOST IN STARLIGHT, before revision (shallow) and after revising with the Deep POV technique. The heroine is writing a story for the school paper on a new guy at school, and she is confused by her attraction to him.

Please compare the two examples…

SHALLOW:

When my last class ends, I go to my locker to get my Trig textbook. I <u>hear</u> the doors at the end of the hall bang open, releasing students for the day and I feel it letting in a gust of air. I notice obtrusive fluorescent lights flicker overhead.

Across the hallway and a few lockers over from mine, I can see Zach and Hayden. I look at a red spray-painted slash on the metal door. I decide that someone must've spray painted Hayden's locker again.

While opening my locker, I notice Hayden's blatantly staring at me. I discern that he is taller than most boys.

I can see he has a messenger bag in one hand, and I notice drumsticks in his back pocket. I lift my hand to wave.

As I watch him, he doesn't return my gesture. He just continues gazing at me with unique eyes. I feel my head go woozy. It even makes my limbs feel jittery. Frustration and confusion are warring inside me for having *any* feelings whatsoever for someone like him. And I wonder why he is staring.

I feel a wave of nervousness because he is watching me. I wonder if there is something wrong. From the corner of my eye, I see him lean into the wall.

I think Hayden's stare is unsettling. I know there's something about that guy's rare smiles that draw girls to him. I decide that no one can resist Hayden Lancaster. Maybe not even me.

I see him watching me, and I feel heat on my skin. I notice Hayden isn't looking at my chest like most boys, which I know will only complicate my feelings for this boy.

So from the first shallow example, could you can see that those extra filter words clogged up your sentence structure?

Now study the revised version...

DEEP POV:

When my last class ends, I stop at my locker to get my Trig textbook. The doors at the end of the hall bang open, releasing students for the day and letting in a gust of warm air. Several obtrusive fluorescent lights flicker overhead.

Across the hallway and a few lockers over from mine are Zach and Hayden. An angry red spray-painted slash taints the metal door. Some jerk must've tagged Hayden's locker again.

While opening my own locker, I'm suddenly aware that Hayden's blatantly staring at me. Hard to miss. He's like a man among boys, at least in his flawless physique. His messenger bag is in one hand, and drumsticks stick out of his back pocket.

I lift my hand in a hesitant little wave. He doesn't return my gesture, just continues gazing at me through those thick lashes that frame his unique eyes. My head goes all woozy. Even my limbs feel jittery. Frustration and confusion are warring inside me for having *any* feelings whatsoever for someone like him. And what's with the stare?

A wave of nervousness hits hard. Is there toilet paper hanging out of my jeans? Food stuck in my teeth? Or have Frankenstein bolts suddenly sprouted from my neck?

Being on Hayden's radar is a little unsettling. I admit there's something about Mr. Puppy Hero's rare smiles, lopsided with an edge, that draw girls to him like insects buzzing a bug zapper. For better or worse, no one can resist Hayden Lancaster. Not even me.

Our gazes lock for just one second, and heat rushes beneath my skin. Hayden isn't gawking at my chest like most boys. He's only looking at my face, which further complicates my feelings for this strange guy.

***

In the second example, I left only one filter word for better flow.

Once you start applying Deep POV to your own writing, you'll know that there are times to use a "tell" word if it reads awkwardly when omitted.

SHALLOW: HEARD

Quote: "Filter words can be difficult to see at first, but once you catch them, it becomes second nature. "I heard the music start up, tiny and spooky and weird," vs. "The music started up, tiny and spooky and weird." One is outside, watching him listen; the other is inside his head, hearing it with him." — *bestselling author, Ruthanne Reid*

"Hearing" is one of the most common senses to use in fiction. When your character hears a noise or the scene changes to a new location, the sense of hearing should be applied for a Deeper POV while describing the scene.

And the sense of hearing can give a character information vital to survival. For instance, it can alert the character to an angry mama bear stomping over crunchy leaves that they might encounter while hiking in the woods, and enables them to get the heck out of harm's way. Writers should use the sense of "hearing" whenever describing a new setting to provide the reader with more sensory details.

Common filter words are *heard / hear / could hear*, which instantly take the writing out of Deep POV. And if your reader already knows in whose POV the scene is written, then why would you need to explain what he/she is hearing?

Whenever possible revise these filter words: HEAR / HEARD

SHALLOW: I hear a scream from the kitchen—it sounds like Amy is scared.

DEEP POV: An earsplitting scream echoes through the house. I guess Amy must've seen Michael's ghost.

SHALLOW: She heard the sound of the car coming.

DEEP POV: The Ford's tires screeched, kicking up gravel on the road.

SHALLOW: Kate could hear the crackling of burning wood.

DEEP POV: The burning wood crackled and spit.

SHALLOW: She heard a strange whoosh sound and looked up.

DEEP POV: A strange *whooshing* came from overhead.

SHALLOW: He heard the stubbornness in her tone of voice.

DEEP POV: There was a distinct stubbornness in her tone of voice.

SHALLOW: They heard another scream, high-pitched and frightened.

DEEP POV: Another high-pitched scream echoed throughout the woods.

SHALLOW: He could <u>hear</u> the roaring of his own pulse.

DEEP POV: His pulse roared in his ears.

SHALLOW: She <u>heard</u> the howl of a wolf.

DEEP POV: The lonely howl of a wolf resonated in the night air.

SHALLOW: I <u>heard</u> the sob in his voice.

DEEP POV: His words faded, but the sob in his voice remained.

SHALLOW: Everyone looked at the field when they <u>heard</u> the whistle blow.

DEEP POV: The game was about to start. When the whistle blew, everyone looked at the field.

SHALLOW: We <u>heard</u> the thunder rumble in the distance.

DEEP POV: Thunder rumbled in the distance.

SHALLOW: I <u>heard</u> the bedroom door slam down the hall.

DEEP POV: The bedroom door down the hall slammed shut.

SHALLOW: Ian <u>heard</u> the soft murmur of voices.

DEEP POV: The soft murmur of voices reached Ian's keen ears.

***

I have included another excerpt from the fourth book in my YA series, RECKLESS REVENGE, which will give you an idea on how to eliminate *hear / heard* filter words from your own writing. The first example has very little "voice" and too many shallow sentences that clutter the narrative and distance the reader.

Please carefully compare these examples...

SHALLOW:

For a moment I thought about casting a spell that would illuminate the yard, but I decided not to. I forced my fingers away from the gemstone and took a deep breath.

Until I heard loud howls from the woods. I didn't think it was coyotes or wolves. I knew this was Northern California. Then I thought that maybe I *should* use my witchy superpowers.

I felt the hairs on the back of my neck stand up. But I decided to stay there on purpose to test myself. I hated letting fear get the better of me.

The night air felt cold and crisp. I could hear the weeping willow tree sway in the breeze. Beyond the back fence, I could see the forest with giant redwoods that soared to heights that seemed to touch the clouds.

Staring into the utter darkness, I felt my palms grow damp. As I watched, every shadow seemed to shift and stretch.

Maybe it was just my fear of the dark, but I felt that fight-or-flight response kick in. Maybe I should run into the house and lock the door.

I heard another howl come out of the forest, and I felt my skin crawl with gooseflesh on my arms.

I knew something nasty was roaming the woods, something angry and loud. I decided to back up while watching the yard for any threats.

DEEP POV:

For a moment, I considered casting a spell that would illuminate the yard, but fought the urge. Forced my fingers away from the gemstone and breathed deeply.

Until chilling howls emanated from the woods. Not coyotes or wolves. This was Northern California. On second thought …maybe I *should* use my witchy superpowers.

The hairs on the back of my neck stood up. But I stayed there on purpose to test myself. I hated letting fear get the better of me. And because I was a control junkie, I had the profound desire to conquer all the things that frightened me…well, to a certain extent, anyway.

The night air was cold and crisp. The weeping willow tree swayed in the breeze, leaves falling from the branches like autumn rain. Beyond the back fence, the forest with giant redwoods—ancient trees, thousands of years old—soared to heights that seemed to touch the clouds. Staring into the utter darkness, I felt my palms grow damp. Every shadow seemed to shift and stretch.

Maybe it was just my fear of the dark, but that fight-or-flight response was kicking in, begging me to run into the house and lock the door. No, more like it was screaming: *Forget being all heroic and fearless and get your butt back inside!*

Another howl came out of the forest, and my skin crawled, ripples of gooseflesh prickling my arms.

Something nasty was roaming the woods, something angry and loud. I backed up toward the house, my gaze scanning the yard for threats.

***

Could you tell the difference in the two scenes?

Did you notice how closely we stay inside the heroine's head throughout the passage, except for that one "felt" verb in the paragraph when I go shallow for better sentence flow?

Although, it is not describing an emotion, even that one shallow sentence could be revised into a much Deeper POV.

As you start to revise your own work, remember that it is easy to unintentionally violate the *show, don't tell* principle when you include filtering words into the narrative, but now I encourage you to weed them out.

SHALLOW: LOOKED

Quote: "Use of the five senses not only tells our reader the experience of our characters at any given time, but can also infuse an ordinary story with deeper layers." —*author, Victoria Houseman*

Decreasing the amount of filter words like "looked / look" from your writing will transform any narrative into an engaging read. The object of Deep POV is to secure the reader inside the character's head without using shallower words that litter your prose and distance your reader.

Also, writers should avoid using "looked" or "appeared" to describe an object, setting or character expression because it is considered filtering (shallow writing). As an alternative, I would describe by *showing* the emotional reaction or the character's expression, or object to keep your writing in Deeper POV.

Whenever possible revise these filter words: LOOKED / APPEARED

SHALLOW: He looked angry.

DEEP POV: His eyes bulged and his lips pressed into a thin line.

SHALLOW: Ally looked at Scott in horror.

DEEP POV: Ally gazed at Scott, her big brown eyes wide.

SHALLOW: Misty looked so stricken.

DEEP POV: Misty wrung her hands and tears welled in her eyes.

SHALLOW: Lydia looked as if she hadn't slept at all.

DEEP POV: Lydia yawned and rubbed at her sleepy eyes.

SHALLOW: She looked less than thrilled.

DEEP POV: Her mouth pulled downwards into a pout.

SHALLOW: Darla huffed and appeared to mull over the offer.

DEEP POV: Darla huffed and tapped her chin as if mulling it over.

SHALLOW: The house looked quiet, almost peaceful.

DEEP POV: The house was too quiet, almost peaceful.

SHALLOW: I looked around the park for David. (Overused "to view" word)

DEEP POV: My gaze swept the park for David. No sign of him on the swings or the slide.

SHALLOW: She looked contemplative.

DEEP POV: She puckered her lips and nodded.

SHALLOW: He <u>looked</u> at me, and I <u>looked</u> back. (Overused "to view" word)

DEEP POV: He gazed at me, and I stared back.

SHALLOW: Zayne <u>looked</u> really <u>mad</u>.

DEEP POV: Shaking a fist in the air, Zayne glared at Bobby.

SHALLOW: Monique was <u>looking</u> <u>amazed</u>.

DEEP POV: Monique's hand lifted to cover her heart and she squealed.

***

Here is another excerpt that will demonstrate how to use the Deep POV technique. The excerpt was taken from my own published novel the first book in the Spellbound series, BEAU-TIFULLY BROKEN. The heroine, Shiloh, is sitting in the car with her mother and they're parked in front of a spooky mansion.

Please carefully compare these examples…

SHALLOW:

I <u>noticed</u> the ghost float away and dissolve, and then I <u>looked</u> at Darrah. Next, I <u>noticed</u> her gaze was still fixated on Craven Manor. But Darrah's face changed in an instant. I opened my mouth to speak as I <u>looked</u> at her, but the hatred I <u>saw</u>

twisting her features made me <u>feel</u> cold. Some old memory seemed to put a wry smile on her lips as I <u>looked</u> at her face, a smile, which <u>appeared</u> painted, suspended over skin. As I <u>watched</u>, she shimmered like an illusion, her expression <u>looked</u> both shrewd and ominous. Her face <u>looked</u> altered, as though her disguise had been removed. It <u>appeared</u> as if her aura thundered.

Her aura <u>made</u> me scoot away. Since my muddled suicide attempt, I could view auras. <u>Looking</u> at my mother now, I could <u>see</u> her aura flare with darker hues. This woman <u>appeared</u> angry and <u>looked</u> like someone else.

DEEP POV:

When the wraith floated away and dissolved within the fog, I glanced at Darrah. Her gaze was still fixated on Craven Manor. But Darrah's face changed in an instant. I opened my mouth to speak, but the hatred twisting her features stopped me cold. Her aura thundered, rolling off her flesh in icy waves. Some old memory seemed to put a wry smile on her lips, a smile which appeared painted, suspended over skin. She shimmered like an illusion, her expression both shrewd and ominous. Altered, as though her disguise had been removed, yet her flawless beauty flickered beneath.

Her aura had me scooting away. Since my muddled suicide attempt—when I'd almost died—I could see auras. Echoes of souls, which revealed a person's true nature, bound in colors that held meanings. Her aura flared with dark hues. She was not the same woman who'd raised me. This was *not* my mother. This was an ice queen.

***

From that last example, you can see that I only used one or two filter words for easier readability, but even they could be revised into a Deeper POV to enhance the scene. Once you start noticing shallow writing, it will get much easier to revise your own manuscript.

Last Tip: Stating that a character "looks or looked" is a bland way to tell the reader that he/she is viewing or seeing something. It is overused, and in my opinion, it is nothing more than stage direction.

Did he/she *gaze, glare, peer, stare, study, glance, gawk, blink at, glower, frown,* or *gape?* Any of these convey more information to the reader. And sometimes "look / looked" or "appear / appeared" is okay to use in a sentence if it improves flow and creates easier readability.

SHALLOW: SOUND

Quote: "I actually like deep POV because I love tight pose. I loathe unnecessary words. Deep POV not only leans up the writing, it digs deeper into the mental state of the character. We probably aren't going to stay completely in deep POV, but it's a nice place to call "home"..." —*author and founder of WANATribe, Susan Dennard*

This chapter will cover ways to eradicate filter words like *sounds / sound* from your writing that "tell" instead of "show." In my opinion, the word "sound" is extensively overused in fiction.

Did the character hear a *noise, hum, echo, thud, reverberation, crash, jingle, clatter,* or *vibration*? Any of which are more specific for the reader.

Not all filter words can be completely removed from your prose because that would be difficult and cause some of your writing to become awkward. If including a filter word like "sounded" in the sentence creates easier readability and avoids passive writing, then I would leave it.

Whenever possible revise these filter words: SOUNDS / SOUND

SHALLOW: There was a <u>sound</u> in the bushes.

DEEP POV: The bushes rattled with a menacing shake.

SHALLOW: I <u>heard</u> the <u>sound</u> of his boots echoing off the floor.

DEEP POV: The heavy thud of his boots echoed off the floor.

SHALLOW: A <u>sound</u> from inside the pantry startled him.

DEEP POV: A *crash* came from inside the pantry, and he flinched.

SHALLOW: The <u>sound</u> of thunder made the house shudder.

DEEP POV: The boom of thunder shook the house.

SHALLOW: He jerked at the <u>sound</u> of his father's voice from the doorway.

DEEP POV: His father's loud voice seeped beneath the doorway and his body jerked.

SHALLOW: The <u>sound</u> of the siren had receded.

DEEP POV: The siren's wail receded.

SHALLOW: He began striding toward the <u>sounds</u> of chaos.

DEEP POV: He strode toward the uproar of chaos.

SHALLOW: The only <u>sounds</u> were the muted muffle of my footsteps.

DEEP POV: The muted muffle of my footsteps were the only detectable noises.

SHALLOW: The smallest <u>sounds</u> resonated throughout the empty house.

DEEP POV: Throughout the empty house, slight noises echoed.

SHALLOW: The only <u>sound</u> I <u>could hear</u> were the rhythmic pounding of blood in my eardrums.

DEEP POV: Everything was muffled except the rhythmic pounding of blood in my eardrums.

SHALLOW: The <u>sound</u> of beating wings was like a balm to his soul.

DEEP POV: The resonance of beating wings was like a balm to his soul.

SHALLOW: I <u>heard</u> the <u>sound</u> of the garage door open.

DEEP POV: The garage door whirred open.

***

Here is another example that illustrates how to revise Shallow POV into a much Deeper POV for your readers taken from one of my short stories.

The first example is before revision and has a lot "telling." The narrative is also cluttered with filter words, and does not have enough "voice." The second example is written close-and-personal (Deep POV), with a more emotional punch.

Please compare the two excerpts.

SHALLOW:

The sound of students loudly talking makes me irritated. I notice Kevin Wells squirming in his seat, looking angry. The kid next to me smells like stinky feet and unwashed hair, making me want to throw up.

As I search my purse for a pen, a weird sound has me looking around. I see the teacher run his fingernails down the chalkboard to get everyone's attention. Finally, I find an uncapped pen, but when I go to start the test, I see the ballpoint only writes a faded blue line. I try it again, but it doesn't work. All dried up, I thought.

Then I hear the sound of the warning bell as everybody finally takes their seats.

Feeling frustrated, I feel a tap on my shoulder. I decide to ignore it, but I feel the person tap my shoulder again.

"Hey, Excuse me, but are you in need of a writing instrument" the boy asks. "Do you need a pen?"

I decide to turn around. It's the new guy from Bio class. I would have noticed the peculiar outfit—long coat, black boots —not to mention his blue eyes anywhere. He is close enough for me to touch if I want to. His eyes look so dark, they appear almost a black color. His eyeballs are looking at me with a frightening intensity. I feel my heart pounding, and feel frozen in my seat.

The sound of a book falling to the floor makes me flinch.

DEEP POV:

The students are making so much noise that I grind my teeth. My nerves are already frazzled from the pop quiz that Mr. Jenkins has sprung on us today.

Kevin Wells squirms in his seat, his ears bright red. Guess he isn't prepared for the test, either. The stench of stinky feet and unwashed hair comes from the boy across from me. My nose wrinkles and I try not to gag.

Ever hear of a shower, buddy?

As I dig through my purse for a pen, an ear-splitting noise echoes throughout the room. I want to cover my ears. The History teacher runs his fingernails down the chalkboard and instantly everyone quiets down.

My fingers touch an uncapped pen in my bag. *Whew!* But when I press the tip to the paper to write my name, the ballpoint only creates a faded blue line. I shake the pen and try again. Nada. Zilch. I slouch in my seat. Dang it.

The warning bell clangs loudly and everybody finally takes their seats.

Chewing my lip, I swallow hard. If I get up now and go to my locker, I'll get a tardy *and* might not have enough time to finish the quiz.

What should I do? Go or stay?

A hand taps my shoulder. I ignore it, but the person behind me taps harder. *Ouch!*

"Do you need a new pen?" someone whispers behind me.

I slowly turn around. It's that weirdly hot guy from Bio class. He's hard to miss, dressed in his usual outfit—black trench coat, scuffed combat boots—not to mention his strange eyes. He's sitting directly behind me. Near enough to touch. His dark eyes are almost black, and he gazes at me with an unnerving intensity. My heart races, and my butt feels glued to the seat.

Why is he staring at me like that? Like he can tell what I look like without my clothes on. I shudder, but I can't look away.

A textbook hits the floor with a resounding thud. My body jerks like a puppet and the noise breaks the spell.

***

The second example has rich details and uses the five senses. There are only one or two *filter words* in that excerpt, and it has "voice" and action and emotion. Even though it is mostly straight exposition, the Deep POV technique pulls the reader deeper into the story.

SHALLOW: SMELL

Quote: "Deep POV is a technique used to get inside the mind of a character and make a deep emotional connection with readers. To do so, the author must remove nearly all traces of authorship from the page. The less that the reader remembers that they are reading, the more effective the Deep POV." — *Kristen Kieffer, writer and blogger*

This chapter covers how to revise filter words from your sentences by using the five senses and omitting the offending words *smell / smelled* from your prose to avoid narrative distance. For Deeper POV, certain distancing words should be removed from your story as much as possible. (However, it is always okay to use shallow filter words in dialogue.)

The sense of "smell" can be a fun way to add depth to your descriptions. Smell can help a character to appreciate the aroma of a home-cooked meal, the whiff of freshly washed hair, or the scent of spring flowers. But it can also be a warning system, notifying a character to certain dangers, like smoke, rotten food, or dangerous chemicals.

One way to write in Deep POV is by incorporating the sense of smell into your settings. Smell is a natural reaction that can be included in almost every scene that you write. In Deeper POV, we experience what the character experiences. We smell the aromas, touch the same textures, and we experience the same emotions, so writer should include this vital sense.

Whenever possible revise these filter words: SMELL / SMELLED

SHALLOW: Suddenly he smelled smoke.

DEEP POV: Billows of smoke burned his nostrils.

SHALLOW: Her hair smelled really good.

DEEP POV: The heavenly scent of her hair—maybe roses—combined with the sunlight glittering on those gold strands caused his heart to thump.

SHALLOW: He smelled her perfume.

DEEP POV: The lingering trace of her flowery perfume invaded his senses.

SHALLOW: I can smell his clean, vital scent.

DEEP POV: His scent hits my nostrils, fresh linen and expensive body-wash.

SHALLOW: The room smells very clean when I go inside.

DEEP POV: The fragrance of leather, wood, and orange furniture polish surrounds me as I enter the room.

SHALLOW: I could smell his cloying sweet cologne.

DEEP POV: The nauseating stench of his aftershave made me want to gag.

SHALLOW: She <u>smelled</u> sweet, like strawberries or maybe peaches.

DEEP POV: A sweet aroma, like strawberries or peaches, wafted from her freshly washed hair.

SHALLOW: A thick sulfur <u>smell</u> was filling one corner of the gym.

DEEP POV: A thick sulfur odor filled one corner of the gym.

SHALLOW: He <u>smelled</u> like a campfire, and I buried my face in his chest.

DEEP POV: His skin and clothes held the scent of a campfire, and I hugged him close.

SHALLOW: The bedroom <u>smelled</u> of dust and thickness.

DEEP POV: The bedroom reeked of dust and a strange thickness.

***

Here is another example from one of my short stories. Try to avoid "telling" the reader how something *smelled / smells* with filter words.

Please carefully compare these examples…

SHALLOW:

Anne <u>touched</u> his shoulder and pointed with her nose. At first, Ryan couldn't figure out what she was trying to tell him.

Then he smelled it. The smell of gunpowder.

He headed toward the smell. He turned the corner down a dark alleyway—and saw his brother Peter lying on the ground with Nathan standing beside him.

Ryan and Anne hid behind a dumpster. The smell of rotting garage and old food made him feel sick. Ryan moved and took a quick look. Peter's aura was gone. He appeared dead. Nathan had murdered him.

DEEP POV:

Anne tapped his shoulder and jerked her chin, scrunching up her nose.

Ryan glanced at her with raised eyebrows. "What?" he whispered.

"Shhh," she replied quietly, putting a finger to her lips. "Do you smell that?"

Ryan shook his head, then the smoky odor of gunpowder filled the night air.

Sniffing, Ryan stamped in the direction of the offending stench. When he turned the corner down a dark alleyway —he halted in his tracks.

No, no, no!

His brother Peter lay on the ground in a pond of red with Nathan standing over him. A handgun rested in Nathan's closed fist. Sweat beaded his forehead. He did not look up.

Ryan and Anne quickly ducked behind a dumpster. The stink of rotting garage and decaying food wafted from inside and Ryan's stomach roiled.

This cannot be happening.

He leaned out and took another peek. Peter's aura gradually vanished. His brother was dead. And that evil jerk Nathan had murdered him.

***

Anytime that you can remove the sensory "tell" from your scenes and clearly state whatever it is the character *saw* or *felt* or *tasted* or *heard* or *smelled,* it will automatically put you into Deeper POV.

SHALLOW: KNEW

Quote: "This [Deep POV] gives you an infinite possibility for characterization and a slew of ways to define character traits without so much as doing anything more than simply writing narrative. And you get all of this because the reader is privy to the characters thoughts and feelings because you've placed them so deeply inside the character's head....The result is prose that is much more snappy, responsive, clean, and clear." — *author, Michael Hiebert*

In this chapter, we will examine filter words like *know / knew* that can take writers out of Deep POV in order to gain a stronger understanding of the purpose and nature of this awesome technique.

Some filter words can weaken your writing and bog it down such as "I knew" or "She/he knew something." Filtering is when you place a character between the detail you want to present and the reader. (I think, the term "filter/filtering" was first used by Janet Burroway in her book ON WRITING.)

Just because filter words tend to be weak doesn't mean they don't have a place in our writing. Sometimes they are helpful and even necessary. So if a writer must state that character *knew* something, then use "voice" and a deeper POV. However, eliminating the underlined words removes the filters that can often distance readers.

Whenever possible revise these filter words: KNEW / KNOW

SHALLOW: He knew his dad wasn't keeping up with the child support payments.

DEEP POV: His dad had stopped keeping up with the child support payments months ago.

SHALLOW: She sure knew how to kiss.

DEEP POV: *Wow.* His toes curled from the soft, erotic kiss.

SHALLOW: She knew he was lying.

DEEP POV: He glanced away when he told her he'd been at the office all day. A sure sign he was lying!

SHALLOW: I know Matt likes me a lot.

DEEP POV: The way Matt stares at me during Trig is an indication he wants more than friendship.

SHALLOW: Derek knew exactly how that would go down.

DEEP POV: Derek frowned. This would *not* go down well.

SHALLOW: When I touched his shoulder, I knew something was wrong.

DEEP POV: I touched his shoulder and he flinched as if something was wrong.

SHALLOW: I needed to <u>know</u> how awful my infraction was when it came to Thomas.

DEEP POV: Thomas might never forgive my infraction, but I had to find out.

SHALLOW: I <u>know</u> I haven't been a werewolf that long, but the full moon <u>makes</u> me twitchy.

DEEP POV: Although, I haven't been a werewolf for very long, my skin gets twitchy every full moon.

SHALLOW: I did not <u>know</u> who would come through that door.

DEEP POV: I had no idea who might come through that door.

SHALLOW: Shane <u>knew</u> his voice was low and <u>angry</u>, but he didn't care.

DEEP POV: Shane's voice was low and toxic, but he didn't care.

SHALLOW: I <u>knew</u> he wouldn't be in French class.

DEEP POV: The final bell rang, which meant he was ditching French class again today.

***

Here is another great example from my novel, DESTINY DIS-RUPTED, on how to avoid "telling" the reader that the character *knows / knew* something with filter words.

Please study these examples...

SHALLOW:

I knew it the second he walked into the room. Daniel, my boyfriend's best friend, was mad at me. I knew I couldn't really blame him after he'd caught me cheating on Trent. In my heart, I knew it was just one little kiss shared with a fallen angel and I'd regretted it the second it had happened. But I had to know if he told anyone about what he saw.

"You can't tell him, please," I said with a whine.

Daniel looked at me for a moment, then laughed. He chuckled and it was full of resentment.

"Okay, Shiloh," he said once he finished laughing. "But I have a request."

My heart felt sick. I knew what he thought of me now. "What?"

He looked thoughtful. "You can do my homework."

"I can do that," I said really fast.

We were both silent. I grimaced and looked around.

"I cannot believe you," he said, looking at me like I was a bad person. "You are not the same girl from last summer. But your secret is safe."

I felt tears on my face. I knew crying and begging would not work on Daniel. He was kind and levelheaded and the words hurt me. But at least I knew he would keep my secret. He was the most honest person I <u>knew</u>. However awful his tone sounded like, I <u>knew</u> the promise was just as strong.

Then he turned his back on me, and I <u>knew</u> he would always hate me.

DEEP POV:

My boyfriend's best friend, Daniel, strolled into the room and our eyes locked. His lips curled upward and his eyes became slits of hatred.

Oh, god. This is gonna be awkward.

He'd glimpsed me kissing that fallen angel, Raze last night, and I had to find out if he had told anyone yet. Mainly one person.

"You can't tell Trent, please," I begged. "It was a *huge*, really stupid mistake."

Daniel stared at me for a moment, then shook his head and laughed. He chuckled so bitterly, I'm not even sure the noise could be classified as a real laugh.

"Okay, Shiloh," he said finally, once his snickering quieted down. "On one condition."

My body relaxed a little, but my heart pinched. "Name it."

Daniel rubbed his chin and smirked. "Do my homework for a month."

"Fine. Anything," I said quickly and bit my quivering lip. "Just, please don't tell him. He's been going through so much lately. This would crush him."

An uncomfortable silence descended.

"Fine, but I seriously cannot believe you," he said, looking at me like I was lower than pool scum. "You're *not* the same girl I met last summer. But don't stress it—your slutty little secret is safe with me."

Tears spilled down my hot cheeks. Coming from Daniel—someone who was naturally so compassionate and even-tempered—the words and his ugly tone couldn't have stung more. But he'd keep my secret. He was the most decent, honest guy on campus. However hurtful his wording was, the promise was forever.

"Look, Daniel—"

"Save it," he said with a sigh.

Then he turned his back on me, and my stomach dropped into my feet.

***

Most of us have heard the saying "*show, don't tell*" many times. In order for a reader to become deeply involved in a story, they must be able to visualize the setting, hear the sounds, imagine touching the objects, and even smell everything within the scene.

These examples should help writers to revise your own stories into great reads.

SHALLOW: THOUGHT

Quote: "If you say, "She was stunning and powerful," you're *telling* us. But if you say, "I was stunned by her elegant carriage as she strode past the jury, with her shoulders erect, elbows back, eyes wide and watchful," you're *showing* us. The moment we can visualize the picture you're trying to paint, you're *showing* us, not *telling* us what we *should* see." — *author, Patricia Holt*

Thoughts can either be shown in italics or plain text, which is a style choice made by the publisher or author. (But *never* use quotation marks for interior monologue.) While italics are most frequently used to convey inner-thoughts, they can become intrusive. Inner-monologue or internal exposition should only be used in moderation when writing in a deeper POV.

However, writers should ditch the filter words *he/she thought* or *she/he told themselves,* which will force the narrative into a Deeper POV. Remember that the objective of conveying character emotion through Deep POV is to anchor the reader inside the character's head without mentioning her/his thoughts.

And if the reader is already inside the POV character's head and reading their thoughts, then they already know what he/she is thinking, right? So writers don't need to include a filter.

Whenever possible revise this filter word: THOUGHT

SHALLOW: I'd better go to the store right after work, he thought.

DEEP POV: If Lacy was coming over for dinner, he'd better stop by the market after work.

SHALLOW: She was still thinking about the party and what went wrong.

DEEP POV: *The party was such a disaster!* Things could've gone smoother if she'd hired a DJ.

SHALLOW: Steven is such a jerk, she thought angrily.

DEEP POV: If Steven kept flirting with her best friend, he was gonna regret it!

SHALLOW: I thought that getting a promotion would solve all my problems.

DEEP POV: I sighed. That big promotion didn't help me financially liked I'd hoped.

SHALLOW: Maybe I should wear this green shirt today, she thought.

DEEP POV: Standing in the closet, she tugged a green blouse from the hanger. *This will go perfect with my new shoes.*

SHALLOW: Let him find out the hard way, she thought.

DEEP POV: She rolled her eyes. Her brother was so hard-headed sometimes.

SHALLOW: I thought I saw Danny cringe at the mention of his dad.

DEEP POV: Glancing over at Danny, I barely caught him cringe at the mention of his dad

SHALLOW: Except for the dragon tattoo on his chest, she thought with a smile.

DEEP POV: She smiled. Except for the dragon tattoo on his chest, he was unmarked.

SHALLOW: A terrifying thought occurred to me. (Cliché)

DEEP POV: My limbs shook and my pulse spiked. What if the killer came back before I escaped?

***

These next two scenes illustrate how to eliminate problems with shallow writing and revise the filter word: *thought*. Please study these examples…

SHALLOW:

Meg thought about what Evan had done. He could so easily lie about it, she told herself. And she almost wished he would lie, she thought, just so that she could walk away without any real heartache.

"Did you really kiss Carrie?" Meg asked, in a jealous tone. "Why would you do that?"

A smile crept over his face, and for a second she thought that he resembled the boy she once knew and loved before he broke her heart.

He shrugged. "Wouldn't you like to know. Sorry, but that's between Carrie and me."

Meg felt tears in her green eyes. "How could you do this to us?"

She never would've thought they'd end up this way—with her feeling so bitter and dejected.

DEEP POV:

Meg's face went deathly pale. She stared straight ahead, eyes fixed on Evan, as if begging him to tell her the truth.

Her stomach panged. *Maybe I don't want to know.* He might even lie about it. But that wasn't Evan's style.

"You kissed Carrie?" Meg's skin heated and warmth radiated from her pores. "*Why* would you do that?"

A smile touched his full lips, his usual smirk, and for a second he resembled the boy she once loved, before he'd met Carrie, before he'd broken her heart.

"Does it matter? We broke up two weeks ago, Meg." Evan shrugged and kicked at the ground with a dirty Converse. "Sorry, but that's between Carrie and me."

Tears sprang to Meg's green eyes. "How could you do this to us? I thought we were going to try and work things out."

"It's too late for that. I'm with Carrie now," he said coldly.

Meg's heart sank lower in her chest and sobs build up in her throat. *It can't end like this. It just can't!*

***

Did those examples spark your own creative muse? I hope so!

As you rewrite certain scenes where information is being revealed between characters, remember that they should still be moving, reacting, and *showing* emotion to keep the pace of the scene flowing smoothly.

SHALLOW: CAUSED

Quote: "First writing rule: Do not use semicolons. They are transvestite hermaphrodites representing absolutely nothing. All they do is show you've been to college." —*author, Kurt Vonnegut*

One common issue with narrative distance is the tendency to try to convey emotional reactions through weaker sentence structures by using filtering words such as "made / making" or "caused / causing" which *tell* how the character reacts after something happens. If you use Deep POV instead, you'll avoid slipping into this kind of shallower "telling" style.

Do I use these filtering words on occasion?

Yes, because I mostly write in first-person POV and sometimes they are hard to avoid without creating awkward sentences. However, my advice is this: if you can rewrite the sentence without it and stay in Deep POV, then do it. If some of the time you can't, then go ahead and leave the filter word in the sentence.

Examples on how to revise shallow writing:

SHALLOW: My heart pounded loudly and it _made_ it hard to breathe.

DEEP POV: My heartbeat pounded in my chest. Now it was nearly impossible to breathe.

SHALLOW: "You look cute in pink," he teased, _making_ me genuinely smile.

DEEP POV: "You look cute in pink," he teased, and the smile that lifted the corners of my mouth was genuine.

SHALLOW: The barking dog was _making_ my stomach clench.

DEEP POV: My stomach clenched. When was that barking dog going to shut up?

SHALLOW: That condescending tone always _made_ my teeth grind.

DEEP POV: Whenever he used that condescending tone, I gritted my teeth.

SHALLOW: Just the sight of him _made_ my heart leap.

DEEP POV: My heart leaped at the sight him.

SHALLOW: When I dropped my ice cream cone, it _made_ her cackle.

DEEP POV: The ice cream cone slipped from my fingers and hit the pavement. My friend took one look and cackled like a witch.

SHALLOW: A shiver rips up my spine _causing_ every little body hair to stand up.

DEEP POV: A shiver zips up my spine, and every fine body hair stands on end.

SHALLOW: The close contact had <u>caused</u> a heat to rise deep inside her.

DEEP POV: He stood too close to her and heat rose deep inside her.

SHALLOW: The weight of <u>disappointment</u> <u>caused</u> Claire's shoulders to sag.

DEEP POV: Claire's shoulders sagged. Losing the football game meant no after party. And no hooking up with the cute quarterback.

SHALLOW: He grips my hips harder, <u>causing</u> my joints to ache.

DEEP POV: His grip tightens on my hips and my joints ache at his rough touch.

SHALLOW: He glared at her with <u>hatred,</u> <u>causing</u> her heart to stutter.

DEEP POV: He glared at her as if at any second he would breathe fire out of his nostrils. Her heart stuttered and she took a step back.

Please study these longer examples...

SHALLOW: The bumpy bus ride <u>caused</u> her to drop her purse and the contents spilled out.

DEEP POV: The bus rumbled down the street, hitting every pothole. She was jostled from her seat, and the purse sitting in her lap tumbled to the dirty floor. *Just great.* The contents spilled everywhere, rolling and sliding in the aisle.

***

Just remind yourself as you revise that "telling" with filter words is shallow writing that removes the reader from the experience that the character is going through or feeling. Anything that describes the narrator's thought or mode of perception is considered *telling* the reader about whatever the characters are experiencing. If you can revise any filtering sentences, the point of view will feel deeper.

To be clear, I'm not saying that "telling" or filter words should be completely eliminated from your manuscript. That would be impossible and make some of your prose become particularly awkward.

SHALLOW: DECIDED

Quote: "Cut out Filter Words. Filter words are a mark of authorship. When you write that a character *thought* or *wondered* or *saw* something, you are taking your reader out of the Deep POV experience. A character doesn't think these filter words while living out their life, so you shouldn't include them in your writing." —*Kristen Kieffer, writer and blogger of She's Novel*

Overusing filter words can have a negative effect on the writing. Filtering puts a distance between the character and the reader, and instead of describing the experience, the filter word *tells* the reader what the character is sensing rather than letting the reader sense it directly.

In Deep POV, writers don't usually need to include filter words such as *he/she decided* or *he/she considered*. These types of phrases can be murder to Deep POV, because they smack of author intrusion. Readers are now distanced from the character, and they are not in their head where they belong.

Examples on how to revise shallow writing:

SHALLOW: I <u>decided</u> to walk home instead of taking the bus.

DEEP POV: Walking home would give me some much needed exercise, *and* I'd avoid sitting next to Loud Mouth Simon on the bus.

SHALLOW: If he had <u>decided</u> on which girl to take the prom sooner, he wouldn't be dateless now.

DEEP POV: If he hadn't waited until the last minute to ask two different girls, he'd be having a blast at the prom right now.

SHALLOW: Maryann <u>heard</u> about the quiz in Trig and she <u>decided</u> to ditch class.

DEEP POV: From the classroom door, grunts and groans echoed off the walls. Maryann backed up into the hall. *Pop quiz?* No thanks.

SHALLOW: Lucas stared at the menu and <u>decided</u> on the turkey sandwich.

DEEP POV: Lucas's stomach rumbled while he scanned the menu. Hmmm, a turkey sandwich sure would quiet those hunger pangs.

SHALLOW: Lori <u>considered</u> dressing as a ghost for Halloween.

DEEP POV: Lori grabbed a white sheet from the closet. This would make an easy costume for the Halloween party. All it needed was two eyeholes.

SHALLOW: Amy <u>decided</u> that wearing pink made her look too pale.

DEEP POV: Glancing into the bathroom mirror, Amy grimaced. Pink was so *not* her color.

SHALLOW: I wanted to go to the movies with Jack, but then decided I was too tired to go.

DEEP POV: I already said I'd go the movies with Jack, but I couldn't stop yawning. Maybe he'd take a rain check.

SHALLOW: The second he touched me I decided I wasn't scared of him anymore.

DEEP POV: The instant he softly touched my arm, my fear dissolved.

SHALLOW: "Beneath all the dirt, he's not half bad looking," the woman decided.

DEEP POV: The woman eyed him closely. "You know, beneath all the dirt, he's not half bad looking."

✳✳✳

Those examples should give you a clear idea how the word *decided* can weigh down your writing and distance your readers. Here is one more that should help. The first example lacks "voice" and it is weighed down with author intrusion by using filter words.

Please study and compare these examples…

SHALLOW:

Callie decided to raise her hand up to the spot where she'd felt the offending prickle against her flesh and touched it, her fingers feeling chilled against the warmer spot on her skin. Something must have bitten her, she decided.

Great. Now I'll die of a spider bite, she thought. But even at her attempt to humor herself, she almost felt tears stinging her eyes.

DEEP POV:

Callie lifted her hand to gently touch the wound where the offending prickle against her skin ached and rubbed it lightly. Her fingertips were ice cold against the warmer spot. Odd. Something must've bitten her.

"Great. Now I'll die of a spider bite," she mumbled.

But even with her attempt at humor, tears stung behind her eyes.

***

Hope these examples help you to revise your own stories into amazing reads!

SHALLOW: WONDERED

Quote: "Choose a chapter or page of your current project and dissect it line by line specifically looking for sentences that can be made more active. Do you have any passive sentences that would be more interesting if made active? Do you have any filter words that are bogging down your paragraphs? Eliminate them!" —*poet and blogger, Carol Despeaux*

Writers should always strive to remove any filter words to deepen the reader's experience. The problem is that a scene that should be active and close-and-personal becomes shallow when a filter word is inserted.

However, if a writer has a few filter words sprinkled throughout the narrative, then they most likely aren't weakening the story.

But are the filters improving it? Probably not. So learn to be ruthless when you can.

And if the reader is already inside a character's head, then the writer doesn't need to state that *he/she wondered / wonder / pondering / ponder* when we could proceed directly to whatever it was that the character is wondering about by using Deep POV.

Examples on how to revise shallow writing:

SHALLOW: I wonder if it will rain this afternoon, he pondered.

DEEP POV: Uh-oh. Those clouds were coming in fast. He put on his raincoat just in case.

SHALLOW: I pondered life's meaning after losing my husband.

DEEP POV: Sitting alone in my room with our wedding album resting on my lap, I sobbed openly. *How could I go on without him?*

SHALLOW: She pondered last night's strange events.

DEEP POV: Too many freaky things happened last night for her to ignore.

SHALLOW: Cassie wondered if Drake was single.

DEEP POV: Cassie flirtatiously winked at Drake. *Hmmm, no ring on his left hand.* Must be her lucky day!

SHALLOW: She wondered if they'd serve chocolate cake at the wedding.

DEEP POV: She walked over to the towering wedding cake. Yum. Hopefully, it was chocolate—her favorite!

SHALLOW: I eyed Marcus and wondered if he had finished his essay on time.

DEEP POV: I sighed heavily. Marcus was going to flunk if he didn't finish that essay on time.

SHALLOW: Sam gazed at the new car in the showroom and wondered if he could afford it.

DEEP POV: The brand new car sparkled in the morning light. If Sam cut back on his other expenses, he could afford to drive that baby out of the showroom within two months.

SHALLOW: I wondered where Stacy was.

DEEP POV: Where the heck was Stacy? Third time she'd been late for work this week.

SHALLOW: Kami wondered why she was always picked last at P.E.

DEEP POV: When the second to last kid was chosen for the soccer team, Kami inwardly groaned. It sucked always being picked last.

SHALLOW: I wondered for a second if he was going to stab Paul with his fork.

DEEP POV: For a second, it seemed like he was going to skewer smart aleck Paul with his fork.

SHALLOW: Lynn wondered frantically which element would be the best to summon if she needed to fight.

DEEP POV: Lynn scratched her chin. Which element would be the best to summon if I need to fight?

***

The following two examples demonstrate first what your sentences might look like with that annoying, visible narrator "telling" the story, and then what they might look like with the narrator eliminated. Please study and compare these examples...

SHALLOW:

Jennifer <u>wondered</u> if there would ever be a time when she could stop being careful. If there would ever be a time when she could use all of her powers. She <u>missed</u> it. It <u>felt</u> like part of her had been numbed.

She <u>pondered</u> if Susie and Michael cared about losing them. They acted as if it didn't bother them, but Jennifer <u>wondered</u> if it did. Living without using her powers was like having a pair of huge wings—but not being able to fly.

There's no point in <u>thinking</u> about it, <u>she told herself</u>. But Jennifer <u>wondered</u> if she used her powers openly, if it might be dangerous like the warlocks warned.

DEEP POV:

Jennifer drummed her manicured fingernails on the table.

When could she stop being so careful? Use her other powers?

Her heart lurched. Without using her magical powers, her body felt numb like it had been injected with Novocain. Almost dead.

Maybe Susie and Michael didn't care about things like that. But Jennifer sure did. It sucked not being able to use her powers anymore. It was like having big, beautiful wings—but never being able to soar above the clouds.

Jennifer sighed and hung her head. No need to keep stressing it. The warlocks repeatedly warned about using their powers in public. They could all end up dead. Period.

***

As you revise, keep in mind that Deep Point of View is only one of many techniques that writers can utilize to craft a story that takes their writing skills to the next level.

In upcoming chapters, I will explain and illustrate even more ways to rewrite any shallow writing, in addition to offering the tools necessary to perform these revisions.

SHALLOW: NOTICED

Quote: "Of course, you want your reader to live the characters' experiences, but filter words won't help you. They're some of the weakest words you can write, in fact, because instead of putting your reader in the character's shoes, you're putting another layer between them." —*Leah Wohl-Pollack, Lead Editor, Invisible Ink Editing*

"Noticed" is a shallow type of telling that can appear in early drafts of any manuscript. I encourage writers to avoid the overuse of the word *notice / noticed* within the narrative. It is considered a filter word, and one that can be easily removed.

By revising the filter word(s), the story becomes much more immediate and intriguing. The outcome is worth the extra effort to remain in Deep POV. Although, some shallower words tend to weaken the narrative, it doesn't mean that the filter word or phrase cannot be used. There are generally exceptions to every rule.

If you find a filter word like "noticed," then also look for variants, such as *noticing, perceiving, detecting, become aware of,* or *notice,* etc.

S. A. SOULE

Examples on how to revise shallow writing:

SHALLOW: I noticed for the first time that her hair was no longer crimson. Instead, her blond locks were streaked with dark purple.

DEEP POV: Her crimson highlights were now dyed a deep purple hue.

SHALLOW: I noticed Diego making his way toward the lobby.

DEEP POV: Diego marched toward the lobby.

SHALLOW: I noticed that there was something tucked inside the book.

DEEP POV: A piece of paper stuck out of the book, and I opened it to read the note.

SHALLOW: I was about to take my usual seat when I noticed that the schedule on the desk wasn't mine.

DEEP POV: Just as I was about to plop down on my seat, I squinted. That schedule on the desk wasn't mine.

SHALLOW: He noticed that the wrinkle between her eyebrows appeared whenever she was worried.

DEEP POV: That slight wrinkle formed between her eyebrows. She must be worried about something.

SHALLOW: She found herself looking at his mouth, and noticed that scar on his chin.

DEEP POV: She stared at his mouth, before her gaze lowered to a scar on his chin.

SHALLOW: Emily noticed Travis stayed right beside her.

DEEP POV: Travis stayed close to Emily's side.

SHALLOW: Hazel noticed my expression and smiled.

DEEP POV: Hazel glanced over and smiled at my expression.

SHALLOW: Halley noticed Isabel smirking at the mascot.

DEEP POV: Halley titled her head and caught Isabel smirking at the mascot.

***

Revising shallow writing and filter words should be one of the last things a writer does on their final draft, but once you become more aware of these filter words, then the easier it will become to avoid them in the first place. There are times when leaving the word *notice* in a sentence is needed, but most of the time it can be removed and the sentence rewritten into Deeper POV.

This next longer scene should give you a stronger understanding of *show vs. tell*. Please study and compare these examples …

SHALLOW:

"Hi. I'm Anna Woodburn," my cousin said, and I noticed her long brown hair tumbled over her one shoulder.

"David Allen," the guy replied.

I noticed that David was wearing a dark wool coat although it was summer.

"And that's my friend, Kristen," David said, lifting his hand toward the pretty girl, who I noticed wore a thin white dress with a long, delicate gold necklace.

"Hey," she said.

"I'm Beth," I said, and looked downward, noticing that I needed a pedicure.

Looking up, I noticed that Kristen's gaze trailed over me as if analyzing my outfit. I noticed a swanky confidence about her, which wasn't all that surprising considering how lovely she was.

"I like your haircut," she mused, touching a red curl.

"Thanks." I felt myself squirm under her touch.

DEEP POV:

"Hi. I'm Anna Woodburn," my cousin said, her long brown hair tumbling over her one bare shoulder.

"David Allen," the guy replied.

I lifted an eyebrow. David was wearing a dark wool coat although it was a hot summer day. Really, really weird.

"And that's my friend, Kristen." David lifted his hand toward the pretty girl, who wore a white dress with a long, delicate gold necklace.

"Hey," she said.

"I'm, um, Beth," I mumbled, and looked downward at my sandals. The polish on my toes was chipped and the skin dry. *Yuk!* I was in serious need of a pedicure.

Looking up, I caught Kristen's gaze trailing over me as if she were a fashion designer analyzing her work. She had a classy confidence about her, which wasn't surprising considering how lovely she was.

"I adore your haircut," she mused, touching a red curl.

I squirmed under her touch. "Oh, thanks."

***

Deeper POV allows a reader to actively participate in the scene and ignites the reader's imagination, as well as helps them to forget that they're *just* reading a story. And a reader who feels like they're vividly experiencing the narrative is a reader who won't be able to put your story down.

SHALLOW: WISHED

Quote: "Filtering is when you "filter" the novel through the character's senses, creating an extra layer of distance between the reader and the story. Unfortunately, filtering is something widely known among industry professionals (it can be a red flag that work is amateur), but it's much less known to aspiring authors." —*freelance editor, Ellen Brock*

Every author's main the job (and goal!) should be to keep the reader "close-and-personal" within the narrative.

If an author can generate a visceral reaction or emotion, and make the reader care about what happens to the characters, then they've succeeded in a Deeper POV. Now the reader will be deeply emerged within the fictional world that a writer has worked so hard to create.

So, I recommend ditching these commonly overused filter words *wish / wished / hope / hoped* that can make your writing become shallow.

Examples on how to revise shallow writing:

SHALLOW: I wished that I could confide in him.

DEEP POV: Staring at Drake, I chewed on a strand of my hair. No way could I tell him the truth.

SHALLOW: Cam wishes he had bought that newer TV.

DEEP POV: Watching the football game on Carl's new flatscreen only drove home the fact that Cam should've bought one for himself.

SHALLOW: He wished he could help.

DEEP POV: He yearned to help the others, but he was forbidden.

SHALLOW: Claire wished things could have been different.

DEEP POV: If only things could've been different.

SHALLOW: She wished that she had a fairy godmother to tell her what to do.

DEEP POV: What she needed was a fairy godmother to tell her what to do.

SHALLOW: Cindy wished that she could go back in time.

DEEP POV: Going back in time would be the only way to fix this mess.

Whenever possible revise this filter word: HOPED

SHALLOW: She hoped Ryan would forgive her before the weekend.

DEEP POV: Ryan just had to forgive her before the weekend started.

SHALLOW: I just <u>hoped</u> I wasn't deluding myself with optimism.

DEEP POV: Now was not the time to delude myself with optimism.

SHALLOW: She <u>hoped</u> he couldn't hear the tightness in her throat.

DEEP POV: Maybe he hadn't sensed the tightness in her throat.

SHALLOW: Grabbing the ax, I hoped it would slow down any zombies who decided to pursue us.

DEEP POV: I grabbed the ax. Now this baby would slow down any zombies who were stupid enough to pursue us.

SHALLOW: She <u>hoped</u> he would get home first.

DEEP POV: If she slowed her steps, he might get home first.

***

This next example is longer and filled with those dreaded filter words that make the writing shallow and create narrative distance. Please study and compare these examples...

SHALLOW:

Dallas <u>watched</u> her emerge from the kitchen and <u>saw</u> her crossing in front of the windows, a bottle of beer in one hand. He <u>thought</u> it was something dark and bitter. Dallas <u>knew</u> she didn't like light beer. He wished now that he'd brought a six-pack with him on the stakeout.

His shoulders felt tight and he shrugged. He felt sweat wetting his shirt as he watched her switch on her stereo. She tipped her head back, closed her eyes, and her body moved to the music. Dallas wished he knew what she was listening to. He had no clue.

I bet it's a soft classical piece, he thought.

DEEP POV:

She emerged from the kitchen, crossing in front of the windows with a beer in one hand. Something dark and bitter. She didn't go for cheap light beer.

Dallas shrugged his tense shoulders, sweat dampening the back of his shirt. Stakeouts were brutal. He shifted in the driver's seat, trying to get more comfortable.

Through the binoculars, his gaze tracked her every movement as she switched on the stereo. Her head lolled backward, her eyes closing, her body seductively swaying to the tempo.

What was she listening to? Jazz, rock, country, or some popular pop song?

He had no idea. Dallas bet it was a smooth classical piece. Light, timeless, elegant.

***

Just to be clear again, filter words or *naming the emotion* isn't always the wrong way to write a sentence or convey an emotion. It doesn't lead to weaker, shallow writing. *Showing vs. telling* is all about finding a good balance.

SHALLOW: REALIZED

Quote: "As a fiction writer you will often be working through 'some observing consciousness.' Yet when you ask readers to step back and observe the observer—to look at [the character] rather than through the character's senses—you start to tell-not-show and rip us briefly out of the scene." —*Janet Burroway, from Writing Fiction*

The primary goal of fiction is to entertain and offer escapism. For a few hours each day while we're reading a good book, we get to be someone else, visit exotic lands, and experience new things. So, to really experience these things, a writer should apply the Deep POV technique. But if your story is riddled with filter words, then the reader will be distanced and unable to experience anything.

Sometimes it can be extremely difficult to avoid filter words when writing in first-person or in close third-person point-of-view. Problems occur when a writer inserts the filter word into a sentence because then the extra words distance the reader from the emotion or action, and they're forced to view events from afar, instead of up close-and-personal.

The two unwritten rules of fiction writing, or should I say, the two most important guidelines to be aware of and avoid are: filtering and an overuse of adverbs.

Even if we think that we understand the difference between *showing* vs *telling*, shallow writing can sneak into our stories. A few red flags that writers can easily search for in their current WIP (work-in-progress) are use of the filter words, such as: *realize / realized / realization.*

Examples on how to revise shallow writing:

SHALLOW: I should have realized that right then was a good time to run.

DEEP POV: This might be a good time to run!

SHALLOW: I suddenly realized I didn't want to be left alone.

DEEP POV: The house was too lonely and quiet, and I had the sudden urge to escape.

SHALLOW: I realized that I'd totally spaced out on what she'd been saying.

DEEP POV: I blinked out of my daze and said, "Um, do you mind repeating that?"

SHALLOW: Alone in her room, she realized that on some level, Mark was right.

DEEP POV: Alone in her room, she sat down on the bed and sighed. Mark had been right about everything.

SHALLOW: They were at the beach, he realized.

DEEP POV: Damn, they must be at the beach already.

SHALLOW: Chandra finally <u>realized</u> the gravity of her faux pas.

DEEP POV: Chandra groaned at her obvious social blunder.

SHALLOW: He isn't coming home, she <u>realized</u>.

DEEP POV: As the sun rose in the east, she sighed. He wasn't coming home.

SHALLOW: Then with a start of <u>fear</u>, <u>realization</u> hit him. It had been his sister stealing the car parts.

DEEP POV: Clutching at collar of his shirt, he groaned. If the mobsters found out it that it was his sister stealing the car parts, they were both doomed.

SHALLOW: I had a <u>startling realization</u> (Cliché) that he wasn't human.

DEEP POV: Stumbling backward, I leaned on the wall. He wasn't human!

SHALLOW: A dizzy feeling swept over me with the <u>realization</u> that I could cast spells.

DEEP POV: Dizziness assaulted me. I could actually cast spells!

These next two examples are a bit longer, and they will give you a clear-cut idea on how to revise shallow writing and remove filter words to turn your stories into riveting prose.

As you revise, keep in mind that especially in first-person POV, there are much better ways for the protagonist to convey to the reader that they're aware of their actions than simply stating it by using words like *realize / realized.*

This next excerpt was taken from my novel, SHATTERED SILENCE (book two) and has a "before" revisions and an "after" example.

Please study and compare these examples...

SHALLOW:

At the Jeep, I fell forward, and felt myself panting and saw dirt rising around me, as I looked back at the clearing.

My breath was ragged and my chest felt like it was ready to explode. For only a moment, I rested against the bumper. Relief gradually hit me when I realized that the howling sounds in the woods hadn't followed me.

What a big coward I was turning out to be, I realized. I knew Evans would be ashamed.

Opening the door to the Jeep, I sat on the seat and locked myself inside. I felt my hands shaking and I realized that it took me five tries to get the engine started. The Jeep made a loud sound, and I felt a breath push itself past my lips.

"Just get home."

I realized that I had said the words repeatedly as I drove home. I wouldn't think about what had just happened.

I was only sixteen, I <u>thought</u>, but at that moment, I suddenly <u>wished</u> I had my dad right then. He gave good hugs.

I <u>knew</u> this was bad. Real bad.

And I <u>knew</u> that I was fooling myself if I thought I was ready to take on paranormals. And I <u>realized</u> that my magick had been infected by Esael's blood.

I <u>realized</u> that Evans was right about my demon brand.

DEEP POV:

At the Jeep, I fell forward onto my knees, panting for breath —dirt rising around me—and stared back at the clearing.

My breath was ragged and my chest heaved like it was ready to explode. For only a moment, I rested against the bumper. My body somewhat relaxed. Thankfully, the howling *thing* in the woods hadn't followed me.

What a big coward I was turning out to be. Some demon hunter. Evans would be so ashamed.

Opening the creaky door to the Jeep, I hopped onto the seat and locked myself inside. My hands were shaking so hard that it took me five tries to get the engine started. The Jeep rumbled to life, and a breath pushed itself past my lips.

"Just get home." I said the words repeatedly as I drove. I wouldn't think about what had just happened. Couldn't think about what had just happened.

Ah, hell! I was only sixteen, but at that moment I suddenly wanted nothing as much as I wanted my dad right then. He gave the best hugs in the world. Hugs that made everything awful seem so much better. Not so terrible.

Because this was bad. Real bad.

And I was fooling myself if I thought I was ready to take on paranormals. Or that my white magick hadn't been infected by Esael's evil blood.

Evans was right about one thing. I had been branded by a freakin' demon.

***

In a first draft, the words can flow out of us in creative mode, but when it's time to edit and streamline our prose, writers should step back with deliberate wisdom and skill and rewrite shallow scenes into Deeper POV whenever we can.

SHALLOW: CONFUSION

Quote: "There are different types of confusion. We can actually understand the emotion better if we read how the character expresses it. Readers are also drawn into the scene more if they can visualize what's happening. And, since your narrator usually isn't a mind reader, it makes more sense to describe it."
—*aspiring novelist and blogger, Teralyn Rose Pilgrim*

This chapter will offer some helpful examples on how to rewrite your sentences from "telling" into showing by eliminating this filter word: *confusion.*

While confusion is not an emotion, it *is* a mental state. Cognition and emotions are closely entwined. Just stating that a character felt confused or was bewildered seems like weak writing in my opinion.

And if a writer continues to state an expression or feeling or mode of thought, then it is *telling* and the narrative can become static and uninteresting. Compelling plots need some conflict or tension within the storyline, and one way to do that is to use a Deeper POV, or a reader might put down the book and never pick it up again.

A character could be confused by the directions to a friend's new house while driving there and become lost, or the character could feel confused about the mixed signals she/he is getting from the love interest.

To convey a sense of confusion, a writer could apply short, choppy sentences, or insert a rhetorical question, but don't overuse the latter. When feeling confused, a character's nose scrunches up, eyebrows knit together, and they frown.

One way to stay in close-and-personal (and there are many!) is to try to reduce as many filtering references as you can from your writing, such as *confused / confusion / doubt*, etc.

Some physical signs of confusion or doubt might be:

Nose scrunched up

Eyebrows knitted together

Staring sightlessly

Unsettling feeling

Hesitate to respond

Briskly shaking head

Licking lips

Tip head to the side

Ask someone to repeat information

Frown deeply

Scrunched up expression

Wrinkled forehead

Scratching head

Blank look on face

Twitching lips

Examples on how to revise shallow writing:

SHALLOW: She was so <u>confused</u> by Hunter's story.

DEEP POV: She scrunched her eyebrows and tilted her head to the side. "Huh? I don't understand."

SHALLOW: He <u>felt</u> utterly <u>confused</u> by the group's announcement.

DEEP POV: He looked from one person to another, with a blank expression on his face. *He didn't get the job?*

SHALLOW: She was <u>perplexed</u> and <u>bewildered</u> by this turn of events.

DEEP POV: Her eyes grew wide. She opened and closed her mouth, but no words leaked from her twitching lips.

SHALLOW: She <u>looked</u> <u>confused</u> and <u>upset</u> by the news.

DEEP POV: She shook her head and wet her lips. "Are you serious?"

SHALLOW: I stare at him in <u>confusion</u>.

DEEP POV: My stomach pitches. I'm unable to digest the words. *Is he really breaking up with me?*

SHALLOW: Feeling puzzled, I gaped at Jessie in confusion.

DEEP POV: I tugged hard on my earlobe and swallowed several times before I could speak again. "Are you sure it was my mom, Jessie?"

SHALLOW: I blinked in confusion. (Cliché)

DEEP POV: I blinked rapidly. My nerves jangled. *Was he for real?*

SHALLOW: Cole's harsh tone left me even more confused.

DEEP POV: Slumping onto a seat, I tried to figure out why Cole was upset.

SHALLOW: I was perplexed by the cat's hissing.

DEEP POV: I shook my head. What the heck was that cat hissing at now?

SHALLOW: My brows furrowed in confusion. (Cliché)

DEEP POV: Blowing out a breath, I stared at him.

***

It is okay to use the word *confused / confusion* at times in a scene; however, you can use it more effectively in dialogue instead of stating it in the narrative. Or if the main character is noticing the emotion in another character. But it is always so much more powerful to be *shown*.

Here is a longer example to illustrate how effective Deep POV can be if you use this method to describe the emotion instead of just stating it.

This excerpt is taken from my novel, BEAUTIFULLY BROKEN. The first version is crammed with shallow writing and filter words. However, the second is a good example of how to describe *confusion* without *naming the emotion*, and it blends "voice" with emotion, dialogue, and action.

Please study and compare these examples...

SHALLOW:

"Really?" I asked in confusion. "Because he didn't seem too interested when Brittany was stalking him at church on Sunday."

Brittany didn't respond, but gave me a hard look. I heard Heather and Elesha snicker. I thought that Heather wasn't as tall as Elesha.

Then I noticed that Elesha had flawless dark brown skin and an athletic body. With her chestnut hair and a thick fringe of bangs framing her angular face, tight-fitting plaid skirt, and blazer, Heather looked overdressed.

"What do you know, freak?" Heather stepped closer and seized my upper arm. I felt her nails in my flesh. I felt her mouth near my ear, her words very cold sounding. "Let me clue you in: guys like Trent Donovan only date girls like *us*." She let go of my arm.

"Oh, yeah? Well, what if I told you he was smiling at me on Sunday?" I lied. Feeling uneasy, I wanted to take the words back.

"I'd say he was just being polite," Brittany said rudely. "Because I've got a date with him tonight."

I felt nervous. My face scrunched into confused lines.

A spark of jealousy boiled my insides. My skin bristled with hate. A strange energy—magickal power—stirred within me. I felt it heat my flesh and flow into my fingers, blending with my anger. It awakened something within me. Then I noticed a dark force gnawing to get out.

DEEP POV:

"Really?" My whole body tensed, muscles quivering. "Because he didn't seem too interested when Brittany was stalking him at church on Sunday."

Brittany stayed quiet, but gave me the stink eye. Heather and Elesha snickered. Heather wasn't as tall as Elesha, who had flawless dark brown skin and an athletic body. With her chestnut hair and a thick fringe of bangs framing her angular face, her gold hoop earrings, tight-fitting plaid skirt, and blazer, Heather looked ultra-preppy and runway ready.

I tried not to roll my eyes. She was attending public school, not a fashion show.

"What do you know, freak?" Heather took two steps and seized my upper arm. Her nails dug into my flesh. Her mouth was next to my ear, her words cold and clear as ice water. "Let me clue you in: guys like Trent Donovan only date girls like *us*. Girls who know how to show a guy a good time. We're *it* at this school. What would he see in a loser like you?" She let go of my arm.

"Oh, yeah? Well, what if I told you he was crazy smiling at me on Sunday? Huh?" I lied.

The words flew out of my mouth before I could think. Maybe I was growing a backbone after all.

"I'd say he was just being polite," Brittany replied. "Because I've got a date with him tonight."

My stomach flipped over hard. What? My forehead scrunched up as I stared at her. Trent and Brittany? *No effing way.*

My insides boiled. My skin bristled. A strange energy—magickal power—stirred within me like a dangerous live wire. It heated my flesh and flowed into my fingers, blending with my anger. It awakened something within me. A dark force gnawing to get out.

***

It is usually better when writing a conflicted main character to *show* the internal struggle through action, dialogue, internal-thoughts, and emotion like I did in my second example. By using Deep POV, the character will naturally convey their true feelings to the reader.

Well, I sincerely hope these examples help you to revise, revise, revise!

DESCRIBE THE SENSES

Quote: "A common writing fault and often difficult to recognize, although once the principle is grasped, cutting away filters is an easy means to more vivid writing." —*Janet Burroway, Writing Fiction*

To write using the Deep POV technique, writers should involve all of the five senses in their emotional descriptions. Try to vividly describe every sensation, reaction, and emotion that your character(s) is experiencing.

Remember that "telling" a reader what a character is feeling or experiencing is *not* using Deep POV. The right way is to show by describing what is unfolding in every scene by the use of action, description, dialogue, and the five senses.

Powerful descriptive writing should always strive to involve the use of every human sense. It is also a great way of making your scenes three-dimensional. In order to do this, I think it's important to stay in Deep POV to construct a more realistic and engaging scene. Because if we don't, as writers, we are cheating our readers by limiting their use of the five senses in our scenes, or by not using them at all.

Please study and compare these examples…

SHALLOW (touch): I <u>touched</u> the dress to <u>feel</u> the fabric.

DEEP POV: My fingers caressed the silky fabric.

If you're going to describe how something tastes, sounds and looks, then you can leave out how it feels and smells. You never want to assault your reader's senses, or they will skip ahead to get back to the action.

There are many ways to achieve Deep POV, but here are a few sure-fire ways to enhance your prose.

THE MAIN FIVE SENSES ARE:

Sight: What your character sees. Describe images and the setting through their eyes.

Hear: Noises that surround your character(s) in every scene.

Smell: Make clear the scents, aromas, and odors.

Touch: Show the feel of icy snow or the luxurious feel of silk sheets.

Taste: Describe the tart flavor of a lime or the harsh burn and acrid taste of whiskey.

***

Below I have provided some examples of the wrong way to describe something and the correct way through use of Deep

POV by including the five senses. The filter words are under-lined. Please study and compare these examples...

SHALLOW (touch): I <u>felt</u> cold when I stepped outside the warm house.

DEEP POV: The chilly winds nipped at my cheeks and I shuddered.

SHALLOW (scent): Lori could <u>smell</u> the trees and pine scents in the air.

DEEP POV: Aromas drifted from the meadow—pine and cedar—as a strong gust blew across the rippling lake.

SHALLOW (sight): I <u>could see</u> Malcolm walking toward me.

DEEP POV: Malcolm strode toward me with a brisk gait.

SHALLOW (hear): I <u>heard</u> ghostly moans coming from within the haunted house.

DEEP POV: Ghostly moans came from within the haunted house.

SHALLOW (taste): The steak was burnt and <u>tasted</u> nasty.

DEEP POV: He bit into the blackened piece of meat, the steak had a charred flavor.

***

As writers, we want our readers to experience the story through the senses of our characters. And by engaging the five senses, plus describing the emotional reactions, it helps readers engage more closely with the character's experience. Shallow writing with filter words can and *will* have the opposite effect.

Please compare the next two examples...

SHALLOW:

When Scott <u>heard</u> the growling <u>sound</u>, he <u>looked</u> down and <u>saw</u> a large dog blocking the trail. He <u>knew</u> it would attack if he moved. Scott <u>felt</u> a sense of <u>terror</u> build in his heart.

DEEP POV:

Scott halted at the warning growl. Standing in front of him was a large dog, flashing its teeth. He stifled the girlish shriek that leaked from his lips with one hand. His heart jackhammered in his chest as he took a stumbling step backward.

***

Can you tell the difference?

In the second example, you can imagine much more vividly the dog and Scott's emotional response. It is always better to attempt to make your scene unique by inserting some of the five senses into the narrative.

Now try to use these examples as inspiration to revise your WIP by using some of the five senses in your own writing.

DESCRIBE THE EMOTIONS

Quote: "Use specific, concrete nouns instead of vague ones like *happiness, kindness, arrogance*, and *courage*. Instead, try to show characters being happy, kind, arrogant, and courageous. Also, use only the most vivid, active verbs, and avoid the passive or linking verbs. Limit modifiers." —*novelist, Maria V. Snyder*

This chapter will include even more great ways to "show" emotion through vivid description without *stating it* to the reader. Try to describe what the character is feeling or experiencing. All well-written novels share one thing in common—character emotion.

The best way to convey your character's thoughts, senses, emotions, and feelings is to *show* them though powerful description. To do this, try depicting the character's physical reactions along with the emotional ones.

Remember to always use the concept of the *show and don't tell* in your fiction writing. This tenet means describing what a character is feeling without actually "telling" the reader or using filter words. Showing takes a lot more creativity than "telling," but trust me, it will pay off by giving your readers a much more powerful and believable story.

Whenever possible revise filter words and *show* emotions instead.

Please study and compare these examples...

SHALLOW: "Go get it," he said <u>angrily</u>, slamming his fist on the table.

DEEP POV: He slapped his meaty fist on the table with a force that rattled the glasses. When he spoke, his voice held an ominous quality. "Get it *now*."

***

Strive to *show* immediate reactions through active physical gestures, emotional responses, clever dialogue, and action descriptors. There aren't any hard or fast rules, but often a character's reaction to something usually follows this order:

physical (involuntary) reaction

emotional response

thought / deliberation

dialogue (internal or external)

purposeful action / decision

If you write a character's reactions in this simple order, it will usually give a stronger visual image in your reader's mind.

Try to keep in mind that *all* plot points, big events, or plot twists should have a visceral, emotional, or physical reaction. Readers need to see a character's emotional and physical responses to almost *every* event that happens in your storyline. If he/she has no reaction to pinch or plot points, or inciting incidents, or overall story problems, then it's as if those actions and revelations have no meaning. If they mean nothing to the character, then they mean nothing to the plot or to the reader.

In most cases, emotional description shouldn't be too specific. The reader should know without being told with shallow writing that the character is, for instance, frightened. It is always better to use stronger words like *shudder, startle, froze,* or *turned away* to show emotions and not use nonspecific "telling words" like *surprise, afraid, joy, terror,* or *disappointment.*

I have included an example of intense emotions, effective dialogue tags, and realistic reactions that are written in Deep POV.

This excerpt was taken from my novel, MOONLIGHT MAYHEM. The heroine, Shiloh, has recently broken up with her boyfriend and this is the first time they've seen each other in weeks. Notice how her inner monologue flows naturally with the external conversation and action—all written in Deeper POV.

DEEP POV:

Then the swoon-worthy Trent Donovan sauntered into the restaurant. My ex with the smoldering eyes—*yeah, I'm a total girl*—and the wide shoulders. Trent with the charming, intimate habit of sweeping the hair from my face. Trent with the electrifying touch…

Dammit. I had to stop going all fangirl every time I saw him!

Still, the air whooshed from my lungs. I closed my eyes and took a deep breath. When I opened them, I swear my body froze. My heart stopped beating. A volatile, insistent thrill shot through my veins, and I shuddered.

Ariana jerked her chin at the counter. "Uh-oh. Ex-boyfriend at one o'clock."

Lifting my head, I groaned. "Maybe he won't spot us."

"Unless you know an invisibility spell, Trent's got natural radar when it comes to you."

My hands trembled in my lap. My stomach pitched and rolled. I had no place to hide. I was tempted to get up and run out the door before he noticed me…

***

Could you see, feel, and sense the character's emotions? Good.

Now open up your manuscript and start revising your own stories into Deep POV to create a gripping narrative that your readers will be unable to put down.

By giving your characters *real* emotions and reactions, it gives them even more realism. Being able to describe those emotions through Deep POV adds mastery to your writing. Add your character's five senses to describe how he/she is feeling without *naming the emotion*, and watch your scenes come vividly to life.

Still not convinced?

By applying the Deep POV method, your writing will become more alive and intriguing. Try it and you'll notice an immediate difference. Your readers will be able to actively relate to whatever your characters are feeling or experiencing in that moment.

In the next several chapters, I will offer some great examples on how to rewrite the most commonly used emotional descriptors. Since this handbook would be thousands of pages long if I listed them all, I have narrowed down the biggest offenders to the most frequently used "telling'" emotions that can make your writing become shallow.

EMOTION: EXCITEMENT

Quote: "Deep Point-Of-View describes how deeply into the POV character's experience the reader is drawn. Regular POV uses words that let the reader know somebody is telling her a story: *Jane thought, Jane decided, Jane felt,* etc. Deep POV just puts what Jane thought, decided, and felt on the page so that the wall between the reader and the character disappears and the reader becomes the character." —*bestselling author, Jennifer Crusie*

Excitement can be felt by a character that wins the lottery, makes the winning touchdown at a football game, or gets asked to the prom by their crush.

Excitement is a state of exhilaration and physical stimulation, which heartens a character and makes them feel a rush of adrenaline. It is an emotion that can add a layer of depth to your scenes if written in Deeper POV.

But within most of the early drafts that I edit for other writers, I notice an abundance of filter words like: *excited, excitement, exhilaration, exhilarated, anticipation, anticipate,* and *anticipated,* etc. As I've stated before, sometimes *naming the emotion* is perfectly acceptable, but only if it helps create easier readability.

Some physical signs of excitement might be:

Body vibrating with anticipation

Hands trembling

Heart swelling

Jumping up and down

Laughing out loud

Hugging people

Bouncing on balls of feet

Rocking on heels

Unable to sit still

Talking quickly

Squealing and raising voice or screaming

Pumping fist into the air

Skin buzzing

Huge smile

Examples on how to revise shallow writing:

SHALLOW: I felt <u>excited</u> and alive for the first time in months.

DEEP POV: For the first time in months, I smiled at everyone I passed on the street.

SHALLOW: "This is gonna be awesome!" he said, his voice thrumming with <u>excitement</u>.

DEEP POV: He was practically jumping up and down as if he had ants in his pants. "This is gonna be awesome!" he exclaimed.

SHALLOW: My heart started pounding with <u>excitement</u>.

DEEP POV: My heartbeat sped up and I bounced on my toes.

SHALLOW: <u>Excitement</u> sang through her, and it was all she could do to stand still.

DEEP POV: Her body thrummed with energy as she rocked on her heels.

SHALLOW: A tremor of <u>excitement</u> crept up his spine.

DEEP POV: He shivered and let out a throaty laugh.

SHALLOW: "So Isaac's going to sit with us tomorrow, too?" she asked <u>excitedly</u>.

DEEP POV: Bouncing in her seat, she asked, "So Isaac's going to sit with us tomorrow, too?"

SHALLOW: Catarina's heart fluttered in <u>excitement</u>. (Cliché)

DEEP POV: Catarina's heart fluttered and her big blue eyes sparkled.

SHALLOW: I felt a rush of excitement. (Cliché)

DEEP POV: A tingle spread throughout my body and warmed my heart.

SHALLOW: His lopsided smile sent a sweet burst of excitement through her.

DEEP POV: At the sight of his lopsided smile, her skin prickled and a pleasant buzz flowed through her.

SHALLOW: She gasped, sending a tremor of excitement up his spine.

DEEP POV: When she gasped, a quivery tremor shot up his spine.

SHALLOW: "I don't believe it," he says with a spark of amusement in his eyes. (Cliché)

DEEP POV: "I don't believe it," he says, his eyes crinkling up into a smile.

***

The following examples from my own novel RECKLESS REVENGE (book four) illustrates how to revise shallow scenes into Deeper POV by eliminating the weaker filter words from the sentences.

Please study and compare these examples...

SHALLOW:

"Tonight sad thoughts are not allowed," Trent said enthusiastically. "At least for three hours."

"How exactly do you intend to do that?" I asked eagerly.

"Maybe like…" He said and leaned over the console to kiss my mouth.

A warm rush of excitement hit me. I smiled at my boyfriend. "Good start."

"Just you wait." He shifted back and chuckled deep in his throat. That's the way a laugh should be, I thought.

Soft music seeped through the speakers and I realized that I was humming along.

"If you like this playlist, I can burn you a mix CD to load it into your iPod," Trent said.

"Sure," I said excitedly.

Trent wore a happy smile as he took my hand and I felt a jolt. His hand was warm and rough. I knew that my smile had widened. I felt my heart pounding so hard I couldn't do anything else.

As excitement bubbled up inside me, I wondered if tonight was going to be fun.

DEEP POV:

"Well, tonight deep thoughts are not allowed. Only fun," he said. "I consider it my duty to make you forget all about your troubles. At least for a few hours."

"Oh? And how exactly do you intend to do that?"

"Like this." He leaned over the console and kissed me hard on the mouth.

A rush of warmth hit my skin. I smiled at my hotheaded, crazy, yet loveable boyfriend. "That's a good start."

"There's more where that came from, sweetheart." He shifted back into his seat and chuckled, a throaty, uninhibited laugh. The way a laugh should be.

The almost hypnotic sounds of *Lifehouse's* "You and Me" seeped through the speakers and I hummed along with the tune.

"If you like this playlist, I can burn you a mix CD to load onto your iPod," Trent offered.

My grin widened. "Yes, please!"

Trent's face broke into that killer smile as he took my hand and a jolt shot through me. His hand was warm and vaguely rough, his grip confident and steady. My heart was pounding so hard I couldn't do anything else. Tonight was sure to be loads of fun.

***

Did you compare the last two examples? Are you starting to grasp how shallow writing with annoying filter words pulls the reader out of the story? Good!

Naming the emotion is a bad habit that writers easily fall into, which focuses the storyline on "telling" rather than "showing."

EMOTION: FRUSTRATION

Quote: "...without frustration, there is no plot. Frustration means that someone is not getting what he/she wants, and that's what makes a story work. Motivation, values, and desires start the character on her/his fictional journey. Climaxes are often provided in scenes of love, battle, or death. But everything in between, the meat of your story, is driven by frustration." —*author at Writer's Digest, Rachel Scheller*

Most psychologists would state that frustration is a negative emotion that occurs in situations where a person is blocked from reaching a desired outcome (goal), or a common emotional response to opposition (opposing force). And frustration can often provoke feelings of insecurity, discouragement, or disappointment.

Ordinarily, whenever a character reaches a goal, they should feel content, but whenever the same character is thwarted from reaching a goal by the opposing force, they might feel irritable, exasperated and indignant.

So in my opinion, a character should be feeling frustrated throughout most of the storyline when their goals get sabotaged by the villain or opposing force.

There is usually no need to *name the emotion*. A reader will understand the emotional reactions, like frustration, without the writer telling them if it is shown. Trust me, readers will be grateful that you are respecting their intelligence.

These offending filter words like *frustrated, frustration, aggravated, irritated, annoyed, exasperated,* can be found in almost every published novel that you read, but should be revised whenever possible for Deeper POV.

Some physical signs of frustration might be:

Brain feels tied up in knots

Talking to inanimate objects

Constant pacing

Urge to throw something

Bunch hands into fists

Snap a pencil

Punch whatever is in front of character: wall, pillow, locker, tree, etc.

Slapping the antagonist

Heart beating more quickly

Breath speeds up

Body shaking

Tapping a pencil or pen

Jiggling keys

Biting lip

Drumming fingers on table or desk

Examples on how to revise shallow writing:

SHALLOW: A bout of frustration churns inside me.

DEEP POV: Pinching my lips together, I stomp my foot.

SHALLOW: The vampire slayer rushed at me with a scream of frustration and buried the stake in my chest.

DEEP POV: The vampire slayer rushed forward with jerky movements and plunged the wooden stake into my heart.

SHALLOW: "No! It's not like that," I said, suddenly frustrated.

DEEP POV: Clenching my jaw, I blurted, *"No!* It's not like that."

SHALLOW: Frustration flicked across Jerrod's face. (Cliché)

DEEP POV: Jarrod snorted and threw his hands up in the air.

SHALLOW: Nikki groaned in frustration. (Cliché)

DEEP POV: Groaning, Nikki dropped her head in her hands.

SHALLOW: Frustration bubbled in my veins. "Accept it. Lisa has a new boyfriend."

DEEP POV: I just wanted to reach out and grab him. Slap him as hard as I could. Instead, I blurted, "Just accept it! Lisa has moved on, and so should *you.*"

SHALLOW: She was <u>angry</u> and <u>frustrated</u>. (Cliché)

DEEP POV: Pulling at her hair, she grumbled, "Just stop it!"

SHALLOW: Jack <u>looked</u> <u>frustrated</u>.

DEEP POV: Jack jiggled the keys in his pocket, and a muscle ticked in his jaw.

SHALLOW: Edward made a <u>frustrated</u> noise in the back of his throat.

DEEP POV: Edward grunted low in his throat and shoved his hands under his arms.

***

These subsequent longer examples exemplify how to modify shallow sentences into Deeper POV by eradicating the filter words from any scene.

Please study and compare these examples...

SHALLOW:

At the start of class, I <u>noticed</u> Holly walk over to me with an <u>irritated</u> expression. "I don't know what the hell you think you're doing, harassing Elden like that," she <u>hissed</u>.

Although I was <u>startled</u> and <u>frustrated</u> by her badgering, I managed an <u>innocent</u> look. "I have no idea what you're talking about, Holly."

She frowned at me in anger for a moment, and then turned away with a toss of her messy hair. "I was just trying to save you some awkwardness, Luce," she said, in a frustrated voice. "He likes me now."

I felt my face turning red. Though I knew Holly was just being a jealous brat, I couldn't help worrying that she might be right.

Maybe Elden *was* just being nice to me because he felt sorry for me. I felt more and more depressed as the class dragged on.

I wondered when the bell would ring and I'd be able to escape.

DEEP POV:

As the warning bell rang, Holly entered the classroom and marched over to me with a nasty twinkle in her eye. "What the hell do you think you're doing? Stalking Elden?" she spat. "Do I need to remind you that he's my boyfriend now?"

My body tensed up and I flinched at her harsh tone. My eyes grew wide and I said in my sweetest voice, "I have no idea what you're babbling on about, Holly. You're not actually worried that Elden might still like me?"

She glared in silence, and I swear smoke was pouring out of her ears. Finally, she turned away with a toss of her windblown hair and sauntered over to her own desk. But she wanted to have the last word. So typical.

"Just trying to keep you from making an ass out of yourself, Luce," she said, in a high-pitched voice. "He likes me now. Got it?"

My face turned red and I slumped in my seat. Holly was just being her usual hateful self. But what if she was right?

Maybe Elden *was* just being nice because he felt sorry for me. I shouldn't let Holly get under my skin, but my shoulders sagged and I hung my head.

The clock ticked slowly and class dragged.

When was the damn bell gonna ring so I could escape?

***

Do a search to find the filter words in your own story if you want to revise into Deeper POV. But remember that there are times when *naming the emotion* or using a filter word will add to the rhythm of your sentences and it is simply necessary, so don't stress yourself out if you can't revise them all.

EMOTION: DISAPPOINTMENT

Quote: "If the reader is in the heroine's POV and she walks into a bar where she doesn't know a soul…she can't look at a man and think, "Wozza, Joe is cute." She has to look and think, "Wow. Who's the hot guy with the tats by the pool table?" She can't see herself blush a beet red. But she *can* feel the stinging heat climb into her face." —*bestselling author, Rebecca Zanetti*

A disappointed character might feel dissatisfaction that results from a failure of expectations, or goals, or core values.

Disappointment is considered a negative emotion that can cause a character to also feel sad and/or angry. The feeling can hover in the character's mind like a dark cloud and niggle at them as the story progresses, causing a dismal perspective. Disappointment is a part of everyone's life, and it can help a character grow and change through their growth ARC.

But writers create narrative distance and author intrusion when they unintentionally insert a shallower POV by stating the emotion. Writers should search and destroy words such as *disappointed / disappointment* and all variations.

The examples presented in this chapter should offer creative ways to avoid identifying this emotion, which only serves to distance the reader.

Some physical signs of disappointment might be:

Mouth turning downward

Tears burning eyes

Tipping chin down and frowning

Heavy sighing

Swaying on feet

Sluggishness

Puckering brow

Leaning on a wall

Dropping head into hands

Shaking head and crying

Stomach hurting

Crawling into bed and hiding under the covers

Weeping in the shower

Examples on how to revise shallow writing:

SHALLOW: He was <u>disappointed</u> that Rachel stood him up.

DEEP POV: Lowering his head, he shuffled into the movie alone. Rachel had stood him up for the last time.

SHALLOW: Bitter <u>disappointment</u> pricked Julianna's chest because she didn't get the lead in the school play.

DEEP POV: Shoulders drooping, Julianna blinked back tears. No way would she cry at school over not getting the lead role.

SHALLOW: Michele <u>felt</u> so <u>disappointed</u> that she'd failed her driving test again.

DEEP POV: Lips pressed tight, Michele dragged her feet all the way home. *Can't believe I failed that test. Again.*

SHALLOW: For the third year in a row, I was <u>disappointed</u> about not being picked for the swim team.

DEEP POV: Looking up with her hands raised skyward, she mumbled, "Why does this *always* happen to me?"

SHALLOW: A stab of <u>disappointment</u> punched Amanda in the gut.

DEEP POV: Covering her face with her hands, Amanda sighed loudly. "This majorly sucks," she muttered.

SHALLOW: How many more <u>disappointments</u> would Alex have to endure until he found another job?

DEEP POV: Tilting his chin downward and frowning, Alex sat heavily on the bed. He was *so* sick of being a jobless loser.

SHALLOW: My voice was low, severe and acrid <u>disappointment</u> tied knots in my gut.

DEEP POV: My voice sounded low, harsh—sour emotions tying a knot in my gut.

SHALLOW: <u>Disappointment</u> swelled so quickly in my chest it trampled the passionate desire.

DEEP POV: Not meeting his eyes, the heat intensified in my chest and squelched the passionate desire.

SHALLOW: A spasm of <u>disappointment</u> hit me hard in the chest.

DEEP POV: My skin flushed. The whole thing was about a hundred levels of awkward and a warehouse full of someone-please-kill-me-now.

***

Here is another example of how to avoid *naming the emotion,* and instead show the character's reaction through the Deep POV technique.

Please study and compare these examples…

SHALLOW:

I <u>looked around</u> me, at how empty the dining room was and <u>felt a stab</u> of <u>disappointment</u>. I <u>realized</u> that Andrea and the rest of my friends hadn't shown up yet to the party.

I <u>knew</u> I had texted everyone the night before with a reminder, but apparently no one was on time.

DEEP POV:

My heart squeezed. *This royally sucks.* Where is everyone?

I took in the empty dining room and breathed out through my mouth. Andrea and the rest of my friends should've been here by now. I'd texted everyone the night before with a reminder.

But damn if I was going to let their lateness ruin my birthday.

***

I hope these examples help you to rewrite scenes in your own manuscript or short story.

EMOTION: ANGER

Quote: "Anger is an interesting emotion because it fuels us with a particular type of energy that demands action, and it can affect characters in many different ways. For some, it clouds judgment and incites violence, for others it inspires an unquenchable motivation, and still for others it pushes them into deep, dark places. I like to make my characters angry for a couple reasons: It's a particularly strong and passionate emotion...." —*YA author, Ava Jae*

Anger is often considered a "secondary emotion" because people often have a tendency to resort to feeling angry in order to defend themselves or conceal vulnerable feelings. But the initial feeling a person has, is actually what is immediately felt *before* the anger. For instance, a character might first feel afraid, offended, shocked, or pressured (bullied), and then angry. Because if any of these feelings are intense enough, it can trigger a feeling of anger.

And anger is one of those negative emotions that can be self-destructive and lead to various problems within a character's life if not resolved. Which makes anger, whether passive or aggressive, a wonderful fatal flaw in any genre. This emotion can be the result of many different factors, like a character's dark history. Letting go of a past hurt or anger at someone within the storyline can be an intriguing growth ARC for a character.

Anger can compel a character to confront someone (like the villain), which drives the plot forward. Or a character might use it as motivation to make a life-changing decision.

Yet it's redundant to be told by a writer that the character is "angry." It is so much more interesting to *show* how the character reacts. In order to show these emotional reactions, try to omit filter words, such as: *anger, angry, fury, furious, rage, enraged, antagonism, wrath, annoyance, irritation, irritated, etc.* from your narrative.

Some physical signs of anger might be:

Face reddens or turns purple

Tension in body

Shouting or raising voice

Swearing / Crying

Punching something

Stomping or marching

Eyes flashing

Mouth quivering

Slamming door

Ears get hot / red

Flaring nostrils

Examples on how to revise shallow writing:

SHALLOW: He looks very <u>angry</u>.

DEEP POV: His mouth is set in a grim line, jaw tense.

SHALLOW: <u>Anger</u> was simmering through my veins.

DEEP POV: Heat licked my skin, and my limbs vibrated. *He was dead meat!*

SHALLOW: My <u>anger</u> returns in full force.

DEEP POV: My fingers clutch tightly at the armrests, my nails digging into the soft fabric.

SHALLOW: A sudden rush of <u>anger</u> surfaces.

DEEP POV: My eyes narrow and my hands shake as I take a menacing step closer to my enemy.

SHALLOW: A red cloud of <u>rage</u> swam across Michael's vision.

DEEP POV: Michael's vision clouded with swarms of dark red.

SHALLOW: I tried to quell my <u>jealousy</u> and <u>rage</u>.

DEEP POV: My body twitched as I stared holes into my friend's back while she flirted away with the boy I was crushing on.

SHALLOW: When he spun back around, his face was drawn with fury.

DEEP POV: When he whirled back around, his eyes bulged and his jaw clenched.

SHALLOW: His face erupted into a map of surprise and rage.

DEEP POV: A vein in his forehead throbbed and he shook a fist in the air.

SHALLOW: She felt an absolute rage boiling inside her.

DEEP POV: An infusion of adrenaline rocked her body.

SHALLOW: Her face screwed-up into a twisted mass of rage.

DEEP POV: With her eyes flashing, her mouth twisted into an ugly sneer.

***

Here is a longer paragraph that indicates how you can revise the emotion *anger* into Deeper POV and engage your readers.

This excerpt is taken from my novel, LOST IN STARLIGHT, and shows both the before revision and the published draft. The heroine just discovered that the guy she's crushing on might be dating another girl.

The first example has too much "telling" and no "voice" and the narrative is weighed down with extra words; however, the published excerpt has riveting "voice" and it is written in Deep POV.

Please study and compare these examples…

SHALLOW:

I am <u>angry</u> with Hayden. "Let's just say last night was a mistake," I blurt, <u>thinking</u> I had better not waver.

Hayden takes my hand, and I <u>feel</u> my heart skip a beat. I look at his face, and <u>think</u> that his eyes are so amazing, but a burst of fresh <u>anger</u> still simmers in my gut.

"Please believe me, Sloane. It's over with Tama," he says. "And I *don't* want to pretend that last night never happened."

I pull my hand away and <u>fury</u> heats my chest. "Or maybe she's more your kind?"

Hayden <u>appears</u> <u>uneasy</u>. "Yes." He glances <u>anxiously</u> at my face. "Sloane, let me prove to you that I'm not a jerk. Have breakfast with me on the beach."

I do not want to be alone with him. I <u>know</u> I cannot trust myself.

I stare at him, and that <u>rage</u> resurfaces. He's such a liar, I <u>think</u>.

While he stays quiet, I try to <u>think</u> of a good excuse. Our relationship needs to be platonic. Because if I go with him, the whole time I'll just be <u>thinking</u> about kissing him.

"Well, Peaches?" he asks. "Can we talk?"

I have no plans today, and I can't even <u>think</u> up good lie. I <u>feel</u> very curious about Tama. But it might be a bad idea.

I know I shouldn't go with him or trust him, yet I feel my rage slipping away. I can't resist Hayden. I look into his eyes and all of the anger dissolves. I know that I will regret doing this.

"Fine." I say, dejectedly. "I'll go."

DEEP POV:

"Let's just say last night was a colossal mistake," I say firmly, resolved to stick to my guns.

Hayden takes my hand, causing my heart to skip an alarming number of beats. I hazard a glance at his face. Bad move. God, those remarkable eyes. A person could die happy just gazing into them. But. Not. Me. I will not be a weak, simpering ball of need.

"Please believe me, Sloane. It's over with Tama," he says in a soft voice. "And I *don't* want to pretend that last night never happened. We had a moment, right? You must've felt it, too."

"Was that the moment you had with me or with Tama?" I jerk my hand from his. "Or maybe she's more your kind? Is she a hybrid, too?"

Hayden kicks at the ground. "Yes." He glances anxiously at my face. "Just have breakfast with me, Sloane, so I can prove to you that I'm not a jerk."

Alone? With Hayden?

Don't do it. Do not do it.

I stare at him, imagining a giant neon sign above his head that reads: *WARNING! Lying-girlfriend-haver!*

While he stays quiet, I try to come up with a quick excuse. I cannot go. I need to keep this relationship strictly platonic. Because the whole time I'll just be thinking about kissing that perfect mouth. His soft, warm lips—

"Well, Peaches?" he asks. "Can we go someplace and talk?"

I shouldn't go, but I can't resist that strange, irresistible *pull* of Hayden. Another look in those incredible eyes and I'm a goner. I am *so* gonna regret this.

"Fine." A sigh creeps past my lips. "I'll go."

***

Did you see how Deep POV brings the scene and emotions effort-lessly alive for the reader? Awesome!

We're inside main character's head throughout the entire second passage and experiencing her anger and frustration, and even confusion, right along with her as the scene unfolds.

EMOTION: SADNESS

Quote: "Emotions are an essential part of the human being. To a degree, we live to feel, and we spend most of our lives chasing after emotions like happiness and love. Emotions are a beautiful part of what makes us human, the good ones and the bad. Sadness is no different. It's part of who we are. Sadness in our life makes the joys seem all the brighter..." —*YA adventure /fantasy writer, Nate Philbrick*

A sad or depressed character is one that would be hard to write, but it would give the story a darker edge to it that might establish a strong emotional connection, or reaction, with readers.

Many emotions are related to sadness such as a feeling of loss, despair, grief, hopelessness, and disappointment. For instance, if a character is sad over the death of another character, then try to find ways to *show* the emotional impact and how it affects their life.

As you revise in Deep POV, you don't want your character's thoughts, actions, or emotions to be *told* or *explained* to the reader because they want to experience the events unfolding inside the character's head as they take place.

So, try to omit filter words like, *sad, sadness, unhappy, miserable, depressed, gloomy, sorrow, wretched, dejected, forlorn, depression, sorrowful, woeful, cheerless* from your scenes.

Some physical signs of sadness might be:

Loss of appetite

Tiredness

Drooping eyelids

Glossy or glassed eyes

Lips pulled down at corners

Sluggish movements

Trembling lips

Clutching blanket, stuffed animal, or pillow

Blubbering loudly

Closing eyes and not speaking

Eyes bloodshot

Dark shadows under eyes

Examples on how to revise shallow writing:

SHALLOW: A sad feeling makes my heart hurt.

DEEP POV: A tight fist constricts around my heart.

SHALLOW: He sounds so sad.

DEEP POV: My heart clenches at his dejected tone.

SHALLOW: I feel sad and lonely now that Craig's dead.

DEEP POV: Sobbing into Craig's old T-shirt, my heart aches fiercely. *I miss him so much.*

SHALLOW: Feeling unhappy, I start to cry.

DEEP POV: Tears sting my eyes and I sniffle, wiping at my runny nose with my sleeve.

SHALLOW: Grief and misery make me feel like crying.

DEEP POV: My arms hang at my sides, my body slack. I clutch at my chest and sob uncontrollably.

SHALLOW: The grief and frustration welling up inside me needs an outlet.

DEEP POV: A surge of pain wells up inside me. Needing an outlet, I grab the stuffed bear and punch it.

SHALLOW: Sadness and loneliness washed over him.

DEEP POV: The constant ache in his chest was made worse whenever he visited Amy's grave.

SHALLOW: I noticed his eyes held a touch of sadness. (Cliché)

DEEP POV: As he looked away, I glimpsed the tears welling in his eyes.

SHALLOW: "Just go away," I said, feeling miserable.

DEEP POV: My face went slack and my voice dull, "Just go away."

SHALLOW: Lauren felt a pang of grief as she went to work.

DEEP POV: Drooping her shoulders, Lauren shuffled into work.

SHALLOW: Jaime just looked at her feet, miserable.

DEEP POV: Jaime stared down at her feet with glossy eyes.

***

The following excerpt is from my book, MOONLIGHT MAYHEM, where the heroine has just lost her father and she is overcome with grief. Although it is straight exposition, there are descriptive details, action, use of the five senses, and emotion laced throughout this scene.

Please study and compare these examples…

SHALLOW:

The sadness I felt made me waver on my feet. I didn't want to faint. When a huge wave of depression tugged at my heart, my thoughts turned back to the funeral.

The grief was overwhelming, as wind lifted the hair off my shoulders. My feet were beginning to hurt in my heels. My best friend was frozen beside me, a gloomy expression on her face.

Another shift in footing, and the <u>sorrow</u> blurred my vision. Wavering, I was sure I would fall over.

Suddenly, I <u>felt</u> two arms wrapped around my waist, pulling me backward against him. A nose touched just beneath my ear, and I <u>could hear</u> his deep breathing.

Trent was here. I wanted to turn and look at him, but only a huge sigh of <u>misery</u> shuddered through my body.

DEEP POV:

Tears choked my throat, burning as they threatened to bubble over and spill from my eyes. I wavered on my feet, sure I was going to faint like some attention seeking diva. With a cotton-filled head, my thoughts returned to the funeral unfolding before my disbelieving eyes. The body of my dad enclosed in a casket that was about to be lowered into the ground.

Sunlight bathed the graveyard in a warm blanket and a mild wind lifted the hair gently from my shoulders, like Dad's soft caress.

My feet were already hurting in my heels, but my best friend seemed rooted to the spot, an agonized expression fixed on her face. Ariana's fingers felt sweaty in my hand, but held mine steadfastly. Neither of us were willing to let each other go.

Another shift in footing, and my mind pulled down a protective screen of translucent gray silk across my line-of-sight. Wavering, I was sure I would find myself on the ground.

Suddenly, two strong arms wrapped around my waist, pulling me back into a solid wall of muscle. A nose buried in the crook beneath my ear, and his deep breathing ghosted along my skin.

Trent. He was here. Now. I wanted to turn and look at him, but slumped against him instead. A huge sigh shuddered through my body.

***

I hope these examples help you to revise your own stories.

EMOTION: WORRY

Quote: "Emotions show up on your body in a variety of hand movements, eye twitches, breathing patterns and more. There are so many ways to show what your characters are feeling without boring readers by saying, Anabelle felt angry. *Yuck!* Show me, don't tell me!" —*author, Jacqui Murray*

This chapter covers how to omit this common filter word from your writing: *concerned / worried / anxious.*

According to Wikipedia: Worry refers to the thoughts, images and emotions of a negative nature in which mental attempts are made to avoid anticipated potential threats.

Worry should be considered a negative emotional trait. This emotional reaction can involve many different fears, concerns, and anxieties that could affect sleep, appetite, or concentration. If a character is worrying about something, they can become counter-productive. Because most worry is based on fear, it can enable a character from solving a problem, or being brave enough to confront the villain. Or even facing their own inner-demons or fatal flaws. Or a character with irrational worries might hinder the hero from accomplishing a goal.

Also, writers should make sure that when they search for the words listed in this handbook that they look for variations. For instance, if the word is "worry" then also search for *worried, worrying, upsetting, upset, distressing, distressed, fretting, fret,* etc.

Some physical signs of worry might be:

Face slackened

Brow furrowed

Eyes darting about in concern

Expression is pinched

Foot tapping

Unable to sleep or eat

Lip twitches

Blink excessively

Clamp and unclamp teeth

Face pales

Expression taut, drawn

Stomach clenches

Examples on how to revise shallow writing:

SHALLOW: I was <u>worried</u> about Brandon being allergic to the new puppy.

DEEP POV: Biting my nails, I gazed into the puppy's cute little face. "If Brandon's allergic to you, I don't know what we'll do." The dog wagged his bushy tail in response.

SHALLOW: I <u>felt</u> <u>anxious</u> and <u>nervous</u> the night before my trip.

DEEP POV: Rubbing my sweaty hands on the thighs of my jeans, I double-checked that I had packed my passport and plane ticket for the hundredth time.

SHALLOW: He was <u>worried</u> that the birthday card had gotten lost in the mail.

DEEP POV: He still hadn't heard from his granddaughter about the card he'd mailed weeks ago. Eyebrows drawn together, he grabbed the phone to call her.

SHALLOW: I often <u>worry</u> about a zombie apocalypse.

DEEP POV: I ran a jerky hand through my hair as I watched the horror movie. What if there really was a zombie apocalypse? Would I be ready?

SHALLOW: The vampire <u>worried</u> that he'd drank too much of her blood.

DEEP POV: The vampire stepped back and wrung his hands. The girl's complexion paled to a ghostly white. He must've drunk just a little too much this time.

SHALLOW: I <u>felt</u> <u>apprehensive</u> the night before my wedding.

DEEP POV: Unable to sit still, I paced the hotel corridor. What if the caterer is late? What if the groom doesn't show up? Or worse...what if after eating that second slice of peach cobbler, I can't zip up my wedding dress?

SHALLOW: He was concerned about the accident on the road up ahead.

DEEP POV: His brow furrowed when he caught a glimpse of the accident on the road up ahead.

SHALLOW: Rachel looked worried.

DEEP POV: Rachel twisted a long strand of hair around her finger, and one leg bounced up and down.

SHALLOW: Cheri sighed, her expression troubled.

DEEP POV: Rubbing at a tic above her left eyebrow, Cheri sighed for the fiftieth time.

***

Next, I have a longer example to give you a better context of how to write in Deeper POV and avoid shallow writing. Please study and compare these examples...

SHALLOW:

I noticed that the guy looked really cute. His eyes looked blue. I was just about to interrupt the conversation when the guy cackled at something the boy next to him said. He laughed long and hard. I moved away, worried that he might be losing his mind. It was the most appalling sound I'd ever heard.

When he finally stopped laughing and started walking away, I felt too nervous to speak to him. But as he passed me by, I got a good look at his orange complexion.

I looked at my friends, baffled.

"Do you think he was wearing makeup?" Jessica asked worriedly.

"Maybe one of those spray-on tans," I said. "How shallow can he be?"

"I know," Amber said, giggling.

DEEP POV:

Damn, that guy was cute. His eyes sparkled like aquamarines. I was just about to tap his shoulder and introduce myself when the hottie chuckled at something his buddy had said. Hooted, actually. His laughter exploding all over the place like a crazy hyena. He doubled over with both hands on his knees and sucked in air with panting gasps.

What was wrong with this guy?

I shuffled backward. Sheesh, he was going to have a seizure at any moment. His horrible sounding giggles were the goofiest and most immature noise on the planet.

He finally straightened and sauntered out of the room with his friend, still wheezing.

As he passed by me, I got a very up close-and-personal glimpse of his "tan" skin. The fake color was virtually orange.

I glanced at my friends with an "oh-my-god-did-you-see-that?" expression.

Jessica frowned. "Was he wearing makeup?"

"More like one of those spray-on tans you can get at the mall," I said, rolling my eyes. "How superficial can that guy be?"

Amber shook her head with a smile. "I know, right?"

***

I sincerely hope that all of my examples help you to revise your own work.

EMOTION: FEAR

Q uote: "To elicit fear...Reveal the menace, whatever it may be, in a place where your character should feel safe, where nothing bad is ever supposed to happen. If your character has allies, you can have them exacerbate things without under-standing they're doing exactly the wrong thing with the best of intentions." —*Pat Cadigan, author of Chalk*

According to Wikipedia: Fear is closely related to, but should be distinguished from, the emotion anxiety, which occurs as the result of threats that are perceived to be uncontrollable or unavoidable.

The negative emotion of fear is commonly related to a strong reaction to something that threatens the security or safety of a character. Fear can alert a character to the possibility that they might be in danger, which consecutively motivates them to protect themself. Consequently, the concept of *fight or flight* is a direct response to feeling afraid of someone or something. And I also think that fears can be irrational or even imagined, like phobias.

Most horror and thriller/suspense writers find unique ways to create the sensation of fear in both their characters, and in their readers. In Deep POV, these types of writers get straight to the point by describing the emotion instead of bluntly stating it.

As with most writing rules, exceptions do exist, but only if using the filter word or stating the emotion will cause the sentence structure to read more smoothly. However, in most cases, a quick rewrite can almost always fix shallower writing into Deeper POV.

For example, try to omit filter words, such as *fear / afraid / terrified / terror/ dread / fright / trepidation / apprehension / scared* to describe a character's emotion.

Some physical signs of fear might be:

Skin becomes clammy

Voice sounds high and hysterical

Screaming

Sweat prickling scalp

Pulse speeds up

A rush of blood through his/her head

A weight seems to press on chest

Body pumps out adrenaline

Hands get sweaty

Trembling hands

Brows drew together

Examples on how to revise shallow writing:

SHALLOW: I feel a brief thrill of fear.

DEEP POV: Trembles travel from my legs and vibrate up my neck.

SHALLOW: She was paralyzed with fear. (Cliché)

DEEP POV: She couldn't move. Until that fight-or-flight response kicked in, begging her to run into the house and lock the door.

SHALLOW: Terror whooshed up and around him like waves.

DEEP POV: His heart was beating at a dizzying pace.

SHALLOW: Terror shot through me.

DEEP POV: My heart thudded louder and louder.

SHALLOW: He was afraid of the dark.

DEEP POV: Staring into the utter darkness, his palms grew damp.

SHALLOW: She was terrified of spiders.

DEEP POV: Her hair caught in a sticky web and she yelped. *Sheesh, I hate spiders!*

SHALLOW: She felt a growing sense of dread. (Cliché)

DEEP POV: A weight seemed to press on her chest, robbing her of breath.

SHALLOW: Katie was <u>frightened</u> by the loud screams.

DEEP POV: Loud screams split the night air. Katie's face turned ashen.

SHALLOW: A sliver of <u>apprehension</u> <u>made</u> her legs wobble.

DEEP POV: Walking stiffly toward the door, her knees locked and she wobbled.

SHALLOW: A sense of <u>dread</u> crept into her heart. (Cliché)

DEEP POV: All the blood drained from her face and her heart thudded hard.

SHALLOW: <u>Terror</u> welled up in his eyes. (Cliché)

DEEP POV: His eyes bulged from their sockets and he started to hyperventilate.

SHALLOW: Tendrils of <u>terror</u> curled into her stomach.

DEEP POV: Her stomach turned to ice and she steadied herself against the car.

SHALLOW: Zack <u>felt</u> the <u>fear</u> clench like a tight first around his chest.

DEEP POV: Zach's chest tightened like a clenched first around his chest.

SHALLOW: The <u>trepidation</u> in her voice <u>caused</u> him to become <u>apprehensive</u>.

DEEP POV: Her tone sounded so ominous that cold sweat trickled down his sides.

***

This longer excerpt is taken from my adult paranormal romance novel IMMORTAL ECLIPSE, and it shows how to portray *fear* effectively in your writing.

Remember that *every* word choice is vital to characterization and to making your writing style unique, so pick strong verbs. For emphasis, I underlined the filter words below in the shallow scene.

Please study and compare these examples…

SHALLOW:

At the <u>sound</u> of the thump, I <u>touch</u> the gun under my pillow. A girl like me living alone in New York must be careful. My fingers <u>feel</u> clumsy as I slide the safety off. Sudden <u>fear</u> chokes my throat.

I sit up slowly, and <u>feel</u> my body tense up. An eerie sensation batters my senses. Beneath my ribs, I <u>can feel</u> an alien power. The <u>feeling</u> is strange, but makes me <u>feel</u> clearheaded. I try to swallow, but the lump of <u>dread</u> in my throat won't let me.

Then I <u>hear</u> a scraping <u>sound</u>.

I switch on the bedside lamp, and light illuminates the room. I get to my feet and look at the closed bedroom door in <u>terror</u>. The hardwood floor <u>feels</u> icy, and I <u>can feel</u> the spread of <u>panic</u>.

I can <u>hear</u> the scratching <u>sound</u> from under the door. With growing <u>fear</u> rising in my heart, I move toward the door. A board groans under my foot and I <u>feel</u> a fresh wave of <u>terror</u>.

The blinds are pulled up, making me feel defenseless. Beyond the street lamps, I can see lights glow in the skyscrapers and notice the winds bend the trees. I feel the brownstone shift on its foundation.

I hear that scraping sound again.

I think it might be an animal or neighbor making those scary sounds.

I feel air move through the room. It fills me with dread. That weird psychic feeling kicks up my anxiety a notch.

***

This next example shows more "voice," action, and emotion by using the Deep POV method. And effectively illustrates how to convey *fear* in your character without *naming the emotion.*

DEEP POV:

I grab the handle of the baseball bat under the bed. A girl living alone must be careful, even on the Upper East Side.

Scrape, scrape, scrape.

An odd scratching noise resonates from the other side of the apartment. The red digital numbers of the alarm clock flash midnight.

I sit up slowly, listening hard. An eerie sensation batters my senses, like a sixth sense awakening, blooming, and soaking through my bones. As it intensifies, the sense of urgency clears any traces of drowsiness.

Scrape, scrape, scrape.

The sound unnervingly echoes like fingernails grating down a chalkboard. I fumble to switch on the bedside lamp, and soft white light illuminates the room.

Staggering to my feet, I stare at the closed bedroom door. The hardwood floor is icy, and gooseflesh rises stiff and fast on my arms. My fingers are clumsy and moist as I hold the bat, the wood heavy in my hand. Whoever's trying to break into my apartment had better think twice.

As I tiptoe toward the door, a board groans sharply under my weight. So much for being quiet. I glance behind me. The room appears empty, but the blinds are open, making me feel vulnerable, naked. Beyond the street lamps, lights blaze from towering skyscrapers and a sharp gust bends the trees. The brownstone grunts and whines against the biting winds of approaching winter.

Scrape, scrape, scrape.

It could just be an animal making those noises, or a neighbor.

The building croons under a harsh blanket of wind. A cold draft moves through the room, reminiscent of sticky breath laden with foul odors, close and oppressive. It feels as though I've locked myself in a dark closet with a hundred vipers.

I force myself to move and hold the bat over my shoulder. My bare feet shuffle closer to the door, then I freeze.

***

Could you tell the huge difference between the two examples?

The first one is cluttered with filter words that caused narrative distance and *named* the emotions. However, the second example gets the reader in close-and-personal because it is written in Deeper POV, so that the reader can really experience the fear in the character as she moves through her apartment.

EMOTION: UNEASE

Quote: "Emotions are the lifeblood of characters and of stories. Without emotional characters, you are just writing events, but you're not drawing your audience into your story. To be a successful writer, you want to create emotional characters so your audience will become emotionally involved with them. It's important for readers and viewers to become completely engrossed in the emotional world of your characters."
—*psychotherapist and author, Rachel Ballon*

Unease can be caused by many different things such as insecurity, anxiousness, worry, or feelings of apprehension.

An uneasy, nervous character might tend to be more aware of their surroundings and pay closer attention to the people around them. Maybe look for exits or fidget restlessly.

Or if the character experiences any doubts regarding certain events within the storyline, they might start feeling unsure, or even skeptical about a situation or about trusting another character. An uneasy feeling could also be a "gut reaction" to something or a niggling suspicion.

Most stories will become a page-turning read if writers revise any shallower writing, so strive to omit other filter words besides "unease," such as: *uneasy, uneasiness, panic, panicked, unnerved, rattled,* etc.

Some physical signs of unease can be:

Clutching at collar of shirt

Wringing shirt tightly

Lacing fingers taut until knuckles turn white

Loss of appetite

Heart feels like it drops into stomach

Nervous tics: fidgeting or rubbing forehead

Cannot relax

Mentally obsessing over a dilemma or predicament

Rubbing (wiping) sweaty hands down thigh repeatedly

Grinding teeth

Tense jaw

Examples on how to revise shallow writing:

SHALLOW: Her panic level shot sky-high.

DEEP POV: She stumbled backward, bumping into a chair.

SHALLOW: A feeling of unease skittered up my spine. (Cliché)

DEEP POV: A cold tremor shot down my back.

SHALLOW: The tiny seeds of her eyes showed unease.

DEEP POV: Grinding her teeth, she blinked rapidly. *No!*

SHALLOW: Panic made my stomach nauseous and I noticed my hands shook.

DEEP POV: My stomach was queasy and my hands wouldn't stop shaking.

SHALLOW: Anxiety overcame me when I checked my bank statement.

DEEP POV: Clutching tightly at the collar of my shirt, I stared at the zeros on my bank statement.

SHALLOW: Dan experienced a moment of body-numbing panic.

DEEP POV: Clenching his hands into tight fists, Dan's body went numb.

SHALLOW: I felt a huge bubble of panic build in my chest.

DEEP POV: Lacing my fingers taut until my knuckles turned white, I tried to remain calm.

SHALLOW: The whole idea of high school dances gave me anxiety.

DEEP POV: I shuddered. High school dances sucked.

SHALLOW: I look anxiously around the cabin.

DEEP POV: Mouth dry and heartbeat racing, I glance about the cabin.

SHALLOW: Maria shot Alexander a panicked look.

DEEP POV: Maria's body twitched and she faced Alexander with wide-open eyes.

***

This next excerpt (condensed) was taken from my new adult romance novel, SMASH INTO YOU, and gives another example on how to incorporate Deep POV by including "Voice," sensory details, description, and dialogue, without *naming the emotion*. In this scene the first-person narrator is pledging a sorority, but she's uneasy and nervous about joining and making a good first impression.

Please closely examine this example...

DEEP POV:

Two of the other girls standing with me in the foyer started squirming and sweating through Jade's rather longwinded speech. Raven chewed on her lip and the beauty queen twirled a strand of hair around her finger.

Jade continued in a soaring voice, "Pledges must obey our every command for the first eight weeks until initiation." She clasped both hands behind her back and stepped closer to the Zeta Beta sisters, who nodded in agreement to every point she made. "Our chapter expects potential members to acquire a certain amount of points to maintain status as an active member. These points can come from attending socials and mixers, participating in philanthropic activities, going to tailgates for football games, keeping a high GPA, or anything that we request you to do. And remember, what happens in-house, stays in-house. Now turn on the lights and let's get to know our legacy PNMs, ladies."

"What's a PNM?" I whispered in Raven's ear.

Raven rolled her eyes. "Potential New Member. Duh."

"Oh."

Interview time. I couldn't let *anything* screw it up. My body broke out in a light sweat, as if a stack of red-hot bowling balls had been surgically implanted in my stomach. I shifted my weight from foot to foot, my toes pinched in my new shoes. My hip bumped the table and the vase of purple tulips tittered dangerously.

The entire room fell silent. I quickly reached out with both hands and steadied the vase. Everyone stared. Raven folded her lips inward to suppress a smile.

A blaze of heat zinged across my cheeks. *Friggin' great.* Now I looked like a total spaz. I shuffled away from the table and demurely laced my hands in front of me.

The lights flickered to life and the Zeta Beta sisters removed their hoods. The members were all from diverse ethnic backgrounds and each wore a warm smile for us. Soft music erupted from speakers hung from the ceiling and a table of refreshments sat near one wall. The large room had sparkling hardwood floors and open stained-glass windows.

The girls mingled, chatting on topics ranging from Greek social events and party etiquette, to cool vacations they'd taken over the summer or unique hobbies. I overheard the pretty Asian girl retelling a story about her recent intoxicated shenanigans and boasting about her sexual escapades. The Zeta Beta sister she chatted with glanced around as if uncomfortable. Definitely TMI.

Raven let out a long sigh. She must be nervous, too. She leaned over and whispered, "The honeymoon period has begun. Better be on your best behavior, Serena."

***

Most scenes can be even more emotional, vivid, and visual if you try to go deeper with the five senses and include physical sensations. Consider revising your WIP by finding ways to make each scene more visceral and powerful through the Deep POV technique.

EMOTION: NERVOUSNESS

Quote: "It's often quoted as "Show, don't tell" because, on the whole, beginner writers do too much telling when they should be showing. But of course it's not nearly as simple as that. Both have their value; the key is to understand their respective strengths, and use each to your story's best advantage."
—*author and mentor, Emma Darwin*

Nervousness might be considered a negative emotional trait if a character is timid or cowardly. Or it could just be a temporary reaction, like feeling nervous about starring in the school play, or a job interview, or going on a blind date.

Anxiety is an emotion that is closely related to feelings of nervousness, but anxiety would generally last longer. Nervousness is a stress emotion, and it can cause a strong physical reaction that affects the character's nervous system and musculature.

So if you have a character feeling nervous, try your best to show it to the reader. Because in order for readers to experience emotions right alongside the characters, they must feel what the character feels at any given moment within your fictional world. "Telling" the reader only achieves the opposite effect of Deeper POV.

I suggest that writers exclude filter words, such as *nervous, anxious, concerned, apprehensive, fretful, fearful, panicky,* or *uneasy* from their scenes.

Some physical signs of nervousness might be:

Facial tics or spasms

Sweaty underarms

Voice wavers / rises an octave

Shift nervously in chair

Hands intertwined with each other repeatedly

Constant fidgeting

Tapping of the foot

Limited eye contact

Talking fast

Trembling voice or stuttering

Sweat beading on forehead

Clenched fists to stop them from trembling

Examples on how to revise shallow writing:

SHALLOW: Piper felt nervous about the contest.

DEEP POV: Piper broke out in a cold sweat whenever she thought of the contest.

SHALLOW: A bout of nervousness struck Kent.

DEEP POV: Rubbing the back of his neck, Kent shifted his weight from one foot to the other.

SHALLOW: A nervous feeling stayed with Jamie all day.

DEEP POV: Jamie closed her eyes and took a calming breath, but it was no use.

SHALLOW: I felt nervous butterflies in my stomach. (Cliché)

DEEP POV: My hands trembled in my lap. My stomach pitched and rolled.

SHALLOW: Claire was too nervous to eat dinner.

DEEP POV: Claire pushed the food around on her plate without taking so much as a bite.

SHALLOW: I felt overly anxious that night.

DEEP POV: I was a bundle of raw nerves that night, my muscles twitchy.

SHALLOW: The closer we got to Grandma's house, the more nervous I became.

DEEP POV: As Grandma's house loomed ahead of us, my pulse quickened.

SHALLOW: Her stomach clenched with nervousness.

DEEP POV: Bile rose in her throat and her stomach clenched.

SHALLOW: Spencer looked visibly nervous.

DEEP POV: Her gaze darted around the room and she jumped at every sound.

SHALLOW: I shifted my weight nervously.

DEEP POV: I shifted my weight, my leg muscles quivering.

***

Sometimes it is okay to leave the filter word in a sentence, but I would advise for Deeper POV to at least try to weed any filter words from your narrative. If you read a ton of fiction like me, you'll notice filter words in almost every published novel, some more than others, but that doesn't mean *you* should do it in your own writing.

Here is another scene on how to avoid *naming the emotion*. Please study and compare these examples...

SHALLOW:

I stood in the doorway and my heart started to beat fast. I felt really nervous. I wondered if the students would notice my rising anxiety.

From the entrance, I saw seven grinning faces staring back at me. They fell quiet as soon as Hunter moved past me into the room. I gulped, my panicked nerves singing.

Hunter faced the kids. "Hey guys, this is the new teacher's aide, Mrs. Beckman—"

"It's only Miss Beckman," I said loudly. "I'm unmarried."

DEEP POV:

I dragged my size nine feet into the noisy classroom and my heart beat erratically. I wrung my hands on my already wrinkled polyester turtleneck. My body broke out in a light sweat as I glanced around the room.

Is it hot in here or is it just me?

I shuffled across the threshold and seven smiley faces turned toward the doorway. They fell quiet as soon as Hunter shouldered past me into the room. I gulped. Loudly.

Hunter faced the students. "Hey guys, this is the new teacher's aide, Mrs. Beckman—"

"It's *Miss* Beckman," I interrupted, my face flushing hot. "I'm not, um, married."

***

Hope all of these examples from my own stories spark your creative muse!

EMOTION: RELIEF

Quote: "I'm a huge believer that mastering point-of-view will solve 99% of common writing problems. If a writer understands POV, then *showing* comes naturally, description is easier to write, character goals are clear, the stakes are personal, and thus stories feel more organic. POV is all about being inside the character. To be inside a character you have to understand that character, and once you understand her, writing her becomes easier." —*author and blogger, Janice Hardy*

While relief is not actually considered an emotion, it *is* an intense feeling that can overwhelm the character. To avoid stating the character's emotional state, like "he/she felt relieved," a writer can *show* a character relaxing or taking the edge off in slower, reflective scenes.

Relief is an emotional response to a lot of different things. For instance, if the character was almost hit by a car, but managed to avoid a collision by jumping out of the way, then they would feel relieved. Or a character can feel relieved when a frustration or fear has been resolved, or they've managed to achieve a goal. Or it could be the feeling a character gets when an invisible weight has been lifted from their shoulders.

The filter word *relief / relieved* can weaken the prose, and I strongly urge writers not to rely too heavily on overused clichés like "he/she sighed with relief." Most clichés like this have been so stereotyped that now they sound weak and boring.

Some physical signs of relief might be:

Shoulders relax

Closing eyes and sighing

Mumbling a prayer of thanks

Sighing loudly

Tension in body diminishing

One hand over chest / heart

Body sags against wall

Throw head back

Wide smile

Clapping hands

Standing straighter

Muscles unwind

Breathing out / exhaling

Examples on how to revise shallow writing:

SHALLOW: Relief flooded her system. (Cliché)

DEEP POV: Shaking her head and closing her eyes, her body relaxed.

SHALLOW: Locating an empty seat on the bus, I plopped down with a rush of <u>relief</u>.

DEEP POV: Locating the last empty seat on the bus, I plopped down and smiled. *Ha!* Lucky me.

SHALLOW: I exhaled with a small measure of <u>relief</u>. (Cliché)

DEEP POV: Sagging against a wall, the tension in my shoulders dissolved.

SHALLOW: Tommy <u>felt</u> a little wave of <u>relief</u>.

DEEP POV: Tommy pressed his palm to his heart and the fast beating slowed.

SHALLOW: He sighed in <u>relief</u>.

DEEP POV: With tears brimming his eyes, he exhaled. *We were safe now.*

SHALLOW: <u>Relief</u> trickled through her veins.

DEEP POV: Softly thanking God, she closed her eyes and sighed.

SHALLOW: I breathed a sigh of <u>relief</u>. (Cliché)

DEEP POV: A sudden lightness struck my senses. Everything was going to be okay after all.

SHALLOW: Cat nearly sobbed with <u>relief</u>.

DEEP POV: Exhaling loudly, Cat swallowed the emotion.

SHALLOW: She'd been <u>relieved</u> that yesterday's fight hadn't ended in a horrible breakup.

DEEP POV: The tension left her body. Yesterday's fight wasn't that big of a deal and it hadn't resulted in a horrible breakup.

SHALLOW: At first, I'd <u>thought</u> he was completely undressed, but I was <u>relieved</u> to <u>see</u> the navy boxer shorts.

DEEP POV: At first glance, his bare torso gleamed in the dim light. *Holy smokes! He's naked.* Another peek revealed a pair of sexy navy boxer shorts. *Whew.*

***

Here are two longer examples, one is *telling* and the other is *showing*. The first one has too many filter words and over-worked clichés.

Please compare these two examples…

SHALLOW:

Noel was so <u>relieved</u> that she'd passed the exam that she <u>prac-tically jumped for joy</u>. She stepped outside the classroom and it <u>felt like a weight had been lifted off her chest</u>. As she hurried down the steps, <u>her heart felt lighter</u>.

***

The next example has been revised into Deep POV, and it *shows* the emotion without bluntly stating it for the reader.

DEEP POV:

A slow smile touches Noel's lips. *She'd done it!* Aced that exam.

She practically skipped out of the classroom, humming happily to herself. She hurried down the steps and hopped into her car. Her head fell back against the headrest and her grin widened. Time to celebrate.

***

These examples should give you some clear-cut ideas on how to revise your own manuscript into Deep POV.

EMOTION: SURPRISE

Quote: "Surprise is a gateway emotion. It doesn't stick around long, so it's almost instantly replaced with the *reaction emotion*, which is the more important emotion of the two. It is important to register the surprise of a character, but it may also be vital for the reader to know what that surprise becomes. For example, if a character is surprised, and then angry, that anger is probably more important to spend time describing than the surprise." —*WriteWorld blog*

While surprise is not actually considered an emotion, it *is* a reaction that can temporarily strike a character when they are startled or something unexpected happens. Alternatively, a feeling of shock would last much longer and have a much more dramatic effect on a character's senses.

Surprise can always be seen in the facial expression, such as raised eyebrows, flushed cheeks, and the jaw dropping open. And it can usually be heard by a loud gasp, squeal, yelp, or short scream.

This short-termed "feeling" can also be negative if the emotional reaction is caused by something like a malicious trick or a scandalous plot twist, where the emotions can range from a slight disappointment to profound shock. Showing the cause-effect connection is critical when expressing true emotions.

A lot of new writers and published authors often name this emotion and use these types of filter words to describe it, such as *shock, surprise, amazement, amazed, stunned, dazed,* etc. I've done it in my own novels, too. However, it is always better to *show* rather than *tell* as discussed in this handbook.

Some physical signs of surprise might be:

Gawk at someone

Mouth fall open

Eyes go wide

Hands flying to cover mouth

Eyebrows raised

Stare unblinking

Short harsh gasps

Nervous laughter

Facial muscles twitch

Cheeks blush

Stagger backward

Inhale sharply

Mouth moving wordlessly

Examples on how to revise shallow writing:

SHALLOW: He was <u>shocked</u> by her outburst. (Cliché)

DEEP POV: Squeezing his eyes shut, he rubbed his temples.

SHALLOW: Remy <u>watched</u> us, looking <u>surprised</u>.

DEEP POV: Remy stared at us with her mouth gaping open like a fish on a hook.

SHALLOW: Ally was <u>surprised</u> by Haley's confession.

DEEP POV: Ally didn't know what to say as the blood drained out of her face.

SHALLOW: Dean wore a look of <u>shock</u>.

DEEP POV: Dean's face paled and he grabbed his brother's arm to steady himself.

SHALLOW: Missy turned red with <u>astonishment</u>.

DEEP POV: Missy gaped, a fluttery feeling striking her belly.

SHALLOW: He reacted with <u>shocked</u> concern.

DEEP POV: Spreading his fingers out in a fan against his breastbone, Jake swore under his breath.

SHALLOW: I looked at Luke with a little <u>surprise</u>.

DEEP POV: My breath hitched in my throat when I looked at Luke. No way could zombies be real.

SHALLOW: I jerked in surprise.

DEEP POV: My body jerked and I dug my fingers into my palms.

SHALLOW: I was shocked into silence by his confession.

DEEP POV: Both of my hands flew up to cover my mouth.

SHALLOW: She looked surprised when he touched her arm, as if she'd forgotten Bradly was there.

DEEP POV: Cheeks flaming, she took a startled step back. She'd forgotten Bradly was still there until he touched her elbow.

***

Here is another much longer example on how to revise your own work from shallow writing into vivid Deeper POV.

Please study and compare these examples...

SHALLOW:

I was shocked and surprised that Janet had actually come today. She didn't even dress for gym half the time.

Cheerleading tryouts had been ruthless, and as team captain, I knew that I had a tough choice to make. It was either my best friend, Bria, or the bigger girl, Janet.

Coach Malkin looked at me. "Who's it gonna be, Lacy? You have to pick either Janet or Bria."

"I'm not really sure," I said and bent down to tie the laces on my sneakers. "Do I have to decide right now?"

"Well, I can make the decision for you," Coach said with a look of concern.

"Okay," I said, brightening and hoping it would be my BFF.

Come on! I thought. *Pick Bria!*

"Bria Harvey," Coach announced.

"Yes!" I shouted loudly.

After a stunned silence, everyone broke out into quiet laughter.

Embarrassment flushed my face, but I couldn't stop the wide smile.

DEEP POV:

Cheerleading tryouts had been brutal, and as team captain, I had a tough choice to make.

Why had Big-Hipped-Janet even showed up today?

Her chubby cheeks were red and sweat ran down her face. Janet leaned over, panting hard like a dog. She was unco-ordinated and at least twenty pounds heavier than the other girls.

It was down to my *very* thin best friend, Bria, or overweight Janet, who was nice, but would be impossible to lift.

Coach Malkin glanced over at me with a raised brow. "Well, Lacy…who's it gonna be? Janet or Bria?"

"Um…yeah…well…I'm not really sure," I mumbled and bent down to retie the laces on my ultra white Skechers. "Do I have to decide today?"

"If you can't choose, it's all right. I can make the decision for you," Coach said softly and squeezed my shoulder.

"Okay," I said and a small smile lifted my lips.

Come on! Pick my BFF! Bria, Bria, Bria…

"Bria Harvey."

"Yay!" I jumped up out of my seat, clapping my hands.

The entire squad stared at me for a full minute of awkward silence, and then everyone laughed.

Oops. Guess that was a little bit melodramatic, even for me.

My face turned fire engine red, but I couldn't stop grinning like an idiot. Bria had made the team!

***

Now you should have even more insight and knowledge on how to revise your manuscript into page-turning prose.

EMOTION: HAPPINESS

Quote: "Happiness is like the color red. It is intuitively obvious but almost impossible to describe without referencing itself. Usually attempts to pin it down result in something pretty vague like, "Happiness means feeling good." —*writer and blogger, Scott H. Young*

This chapter will cover how to show *happiness / joy* without actually stating the emotion for the reader. The word "happy" can convey many differing emotions such as, excitement, enthusiasm, or animation.

Happiness could be considered a feeling *and* an emotion. Joy is a mental or emotional state of well-being distinguished by positive or pleasant feelings ranging from relaxed contentment to overwhelming exhilaration.

To be honest, characters that are happy are...well, boring. Now a writer *could* show a character feeling happy on the first page or two, but then something terrible or dire, like an inciting incident, better happen pretty quickly to quell this happy character's life in some big way. That's why conflict and tension make such page-turning reads. Characters generally shouldn't get their happy ending until the end of the story. And make them work for it...

Also, I'm not saying you cannot use the word "happy," if it is appropriate, but writers should try to revise any scenes without *naming the emotion.*

Some physical signs of happiness might be:

Eyes sparkling

Feeling of lightness

Bouncing on toes

Swinging arms

Explosion of endorphins

Laughing / giggling

Hugging him/herself

Skin glowing

Cheering and squealing

Hyper aware of surroundings

Singing or humming to him/herself

Voice high-pitched or shrieking

Examples on how to revise shallow writing:

SHALLOW: A flood of happiness poured through me. (Cliché)

DEEP POV: Swinging my arms while walking home, I couldn't stop grinning.

SHALLOW: She was so happy that she'd won the new car.

DEEP POV: Bouncing on her toes, she clutched the keys to her new car in one hand. "This is the best day of my life!" she exclaimed and hugged the stranger standing next to her.

SHALLOW: Elizabeth wanted to jump for joy. (Cliché)

DEEP POV: Holding both of her arms out wide as if she could hug the entire world, Elizabeth beamed at her husband. A second honeymoon sounded awesome.

SHALLOW: A sense of joy bubbled up in her heart.

DEEP POV: A sense of weightlessness struck her heart. She rubbed her cheeks, her face hurting from the wide grin that lifted her lips.

SHALLOW: "That's great news!" I cried happily.

DEEP POV: If my smile became any wider, I'd resemble the Joker. "Great news!"

SHALLOW: Sandy actually squealed in happiness.

DEEP POV: "Yay!" Sandy giggled uncontrollably and clapped her hands. "Let's party!"

SHALLOW: I felt happy when Sam told me the good news.

DEEP POV: A big goofy grin pulled at my mouth when Sam told me the good news.

SHALLOW: I'd never felt so happy to see the first rays of dawn in my life.

DEEP POV: As the first rays of dawn peeked through the blinds, I threw my arms wide.

SHALLOW: I sighed with true happiness.

DEEP POV: A sigh escaped and I beamed.

SHALLOW: I thought I might just die from happiness. (Cliché)

DEEP POV: Dancing around wildly, a bubbly sensation filled my heart.

***

This longer example illustrates how to revise "telling" sentences and filter words into *showing*. Again, it is fine to occasionally use the words *joy / happiness* in your writing, but if it's possible not to—then don't.

Please study and compare these examples…

SHALLOW:

Damon wrapped his arms around me, and then I felt him put his lips to mine. I felt a thrill of profound happiness as Damon stroked my back. I felt my heartbeat quicken.

But Damon wasn't a very good kisser. Maybe my friend Mindy could provide some instruction.

Damon pulled back. "I'll call you later, okay?"

I realized I had his slobber on my chin. "Sure." I stood there watching as the pickup drove away.

When the taillights had almost vanished into the darkness, I headed toward the porch. I felt my heart lift with joy, even though I knew the kiss had been awful.

***

I have included "voice," emotion, and dialogue in my next example to give you a better idea of how to redraft scenes in your own work.

DEEP POV:

Damon wrapped his arms around my waist and pulled me closer. My breath hitched in my throat. For a moment, a warm thrill shot through my body when his soft lips touched mine.

Yuk. Too sloppy.

But hopefully this kissing stuff would get better with lots and lots of practice. Maybe I could borrow Mindy's book on *Twenty-Five Ways to Be a Great Lover*. That girl had to be a professional, the way she was always practicing her kissing techniques on her pillow.

Damon pulled back and smiled. "I gotta get going. Call you later, okay?"

Trying not to act grossed out that his slobber was wetting my chin, I said, "Yeah. Sure."

I grinned like a big doofus until the truck pulled away. When the taillights faded into the night, I skipped onto the porch, swirling the hem of my skirt back and forth like a little girl.

Wow. *My first real kiss.* What a disaster! But also all kinds of awesome.

***

Now I challenge you to rewrite a scene in your own novel or story where the characters experience true happiness and *show* it.

EMOTION: JEALOUSLY

Quote: "While I believe excessive jealousy falls into the category of emotional and mental abuse, I also think we have (most of us) felt jealous over something. Even if we're not talking about romantic relationships. For example, being jealous about your best friend talking very excitedly to someone else. Jealousy is a natural emotion just like love and anger. And it doesn't always have to be negative. It's how you react to the feeling of jealousy that shows whether it is a healthy or unhealthy reaction." —*Alex, Reference for Writers blog*

Everyone feels jealously at some point in their lives. Even I've felt envy over another writer's success, although sometimes it is hard not to feel that way.

Envy characteristically refers to the negative thoughts and feelings of other emotions such as self-doubt, apprehension, worry, and anxiety. It is a strong negative emotion that can affect friendships, family, and all other relationships.

A good storyline could include a character that starts off being jealous as a fatal flaw in some fictional world riddled with envy and greed, which are caused by a cutthroat, consumer-driven culture. This same character could overcome this feeling during his growth ARC and no longer feel jealous of others or circumstances. Or the character could be dealing with feelings of jealousy over a lover, and they need to conquer this insecure emotion within the storyline before the love interest decides to dump them.

In almost every scene, I think it's important to stay in Deep POV. As you revise, remember that there are a dozen different ways to describe a physical, internal, or emotional response. And by using the tips and tools in this book as a guide, you'll discover some interesting things about your characters.

Writer should eliminate the filter words: *jealousy, envy, envious, wariness, mistrustfulness, resentment, resentfulness, spite, begrudge* from your narrative.

Some physical signs of envy might be:

Breath harsh and shallow

Hands curling into fists at sides

Teeth clenched

Chest puffs out / heats up

Heart lurches

Burning sensation in chest

Wanting to cry

Crossing arms

Tight muscles

Quick toss of head

Voice low, snarky

Body tenses up

Examples on how to revise shallow writing:

SHALLOW: Darren was green with <u>jealousy</u>. (Cliché)

DEEP POV: Shoving the hair from his eyes, Darren stomped inside the house. The nerve of Tom flashing his new lawn-mower in front of all the neighbors. But damn, that machine was cool looking.

SHALLOW:

Tom <u>feels</u> a strong flare of <u>jealousy</u>.

DEEP POV:

Tom stares hard at his best friend and the girl he's crushing on. His hands curl into fists at his sides, itching to swing out and put a dent in the wall beside him. *She's my girl!*

SHALLOW: A spark of <u>jealousy</u> struck my heart.

DEEP POV: A pang struck my heart. How could Krystal buy the same dress I'd been drooling over for weeks? And the gown looked better on her than me.

SHALLOW: There was an edge of <u>jealousy</u> in my own voice.

DEEP POV: Clenching my teeth, I snapped, "I always *knew* you liked her better!"

SHALLOW: I tried very hard not to envy her.

DEEP POV: My best friend was beyond spoiled. New car. Expensive apartment. Trust fund. And she took it all for granted while I slaved away working double-shifts for minimum wage.

SHALLOW: Feeling a stab of envy, Christina glared at Yolanda.

DEEP POV: A burning sensation stabbed Christina in the chest. Yolanda thought she was *so* special with her new haircut and designer purse. Ha! That bag was a cheap knockoff and she'd prove it.

SHALLOW: I can't contain my envy.

DEEP POV: My eyes narrow. My breaths come out coarser as I stare down at the gifts under the lighted tree. *So unfair!* Jonathon always got ten times more Christmas presents than me.

SHALLOW: I felt jealousy growing inside me.

DEEP POV: Huffing, I tried to contain the green monster growling inside me, but failed. "Your book is on the bestseller's list *again?*" I spat. Mine hadn't even made *Amazon's Top 100*.

SHALLOW: Hot jealousy colored her dark tone.

DEEP POV: Her ugly tone luridly colored her accusation and I half-expected her breath to come out in little green puffs.

SHALLOW: Dean's <u>jealous</u> grip on me tightened. "Are you cheating on me?"

DEEP POV: Dean's grip tightened on my arm and his neck muscles bunched up. "Are you cheating on me?"

SHALLOW: <u>Envy</u> oozed from him in waves when he <u>saw</u> his ex with another man.

DEEP POV: His chest puffed out and his movements stiffened when he spotted his ex with that tall dude.

***

In this next illustration, I show how using deeper narration and vivid emotion allows you to effectively turn your shallow scene into a deeper reading experience for your readers.

Please study and compare these examples…

SHALLOW:

I <u>felt</u> green with <u>jealousy</u>. There was something wrong with me. I had my own boyfriend, but I wanted to be with hers. I already <u>knew</u> Kyle was cute and sexy and nice. I <u>wished</u> that he'd seen me first.

"Wanna see another picture of Kyle at the beach?" Tamara asked sweetly.

"Sure," I said, <u>jealousy</u> tainting my voice.

She didn't <u>notice</u> as she scrolled to a photo of Kyle taken on her iPhone. I <u>thought</u> he <u>looked</u> very handsome in shorts and shirtless, his big smile, and his tousled dark hair.

My heart panged again with growing <u>envy</u>.

DEEP POV:

Pursing my lips into a flat, hard line, I tried to ignore the way my body flushed hot and cold. *What's wrong with me?*

My best friend was showing off pics of her hot new boyfriend, and instead of being happy for her, it made my own boyfriend seem like a boring nerd.

How selfish could I be?

"Wanna see another picture of Kyle at the beach?" Tamara asked with a smile.

No. I really, really *didn't* want to keep looking at photos of her perfect boyfriend.

Taking a step closer, fists clenched, I muttered, "Yeah...I guess."

Tamara smiled and handed me her iPhone. In the photo, Kyle looked insanely hot in board shorts with no shirt, his muscled chest sprinkled with salt water and his black hair tousled from the wind.

Damn, he was a hottie. And unfortunately, all *hers.*

***

A good thing to remember as you revise a scene into Deeper POV is that male and female characters should react, experience, communicate, and convey feelings differently. When writing a character of the opposite sex in Deep POV, try to get a second opinion by a beta reader or critique partner to ensure that the male and female character reactions, responses, and emotions are written realistically.

EMOTION: EMBARRASSMENT

Quote: "Counselors tell us that thoughts lead to emotions, and emotions lead to actions. As a writer, you can easily show your character's thoughts and actions. Readers are smart enough to deduce the emotions based on what the characters think and do. So often it seems writers are in a hurry. When you have a very emotional scene, slow it down. Let us hear your character's every thought. Highlight a few details. Show the actions." —*novelist and writing coach, C. S. Lakin*

This chapter provides a few examples on ways to show a character's embarrassing moments through a Deeper POV. For instance, when a character feels embarrassment the neck, ears, and face may appear flushed and the skin colors a reddish hue.

Embarrassment is considered a complex emotion and a universal feeling that everyone can easily relate to. It is a self-conscious reaction tied to other emotions such as insecurity (low self-esteem), self-judgment, and social discomfort, etc.

Humiliations are usually the direct result of unintentional behaviors that cause feelings of negativity about oneself—even when a person had no intent of breaking any number of so-called social standards.

For each scene, identify the emotion that your character needs to *show* and think of different ways you can reinforce the character's reactions through both verbal and nonverbal communication. One way is to omit filter words like *embarrassed, embarrassment, self-conscious, ashamed, mortified, humiliated, humiliation,* or *shame* from your writing.

Some physical signs of embarrassment might be:

Stomach roiling

Faintness

Feeling the urge to pee

Legs quivering

Swallowing hard

Voice squeaks

Glancing around at surroundings

Not making eye contact

Backing away or running away

Hiding face in hair

Leg bouncing

Tugging at eyebrow / earlobe

Examples on how to revise shallow writing:

SHALLOW: Feeling embarrassed, I jerked back.

DEEP POV: Jerking back, my neck turned red and I was breathing hard.

SHALLOW: I was actually <u>embarrassed</u> that he wanted to display that kind of affection in plain view of everyone.

DEEP POV: My cheeks flushed pink. *PDA in the cafeteria?* No. Thanks.

SHALLOW: I was so <u>embarrassed</u> that I wanted to run and hide. (Cliché)

DEEP POV: If the ground opened up and swallowed me right now, I'd be a happy camper.

SHALLOW: "I'm not going!" she said, <u>embarrassed</u> to be treated like a child.

DEEP POV: "I'm not going!" she snapped, a bloom of heat staining her neck and ears. She was almost eighteen! Her parents couldn't keep treating her like a child.

SHALLOW: I tucked my hands under my butt, feeling <u>embarrassed</u>.

DEEP POV: I tucked my fidgety hands under my butt.

SHALLOW: I looked at the ground in <u>embarrassment</u>.

DEEP POV: Staring at my feet, I worked to steady my own breathing.

SHALLOW: I got that squirmy, <u>embarrassed</u> feeling that awkward conversations with parents can bring about.

DEEP POV: I got a squirmy feeling in my gut and shifted in my seat. This conversation with my parents was gonna be all kinds of awkward.

SHALLOW: An <u>embarrassed</u> blush stained my cheeks.

DEEP POV: A hot flush stained my cheeks.

SHALLOW: I took a deep breath and held it, squelching a <u>humiliated</u> giggle.

DEEP POV: Taking a deep breath, I held it in to stifle the unwelcome giggle.

SHALLOW: <u>Embarrassed</u>, I muttered, "Aren't you going to kiss me good night?"

DEEP POV: My heartbeat turned unruly and my voice became husky. "Aren't you going to kiss me good night?"

SHALLOW: She looked down, <u>feeling embarrassed</u>, but he pulled her chin up, turning her head so that she met his eyes.

DEEP POV: She turned away, her collarbone hot, but he pulled her chin up, turning her head so that she met his eyes.

***

These next scenes are written in both Shallow POV and Deep POV to exemplify how to revise sentences, paragraphs, and scenes in your own work.

This excerpt is taken from my novel, IMMORTAL ECLIPSE and the *shallow* example is an early draft before revision. In this excerpt, the heroine is meeting the love interest for the first time.

Please study and compare these examples...

SHALLOW:

As we stand there looking at each other, I feel a thrilling sensation and now I feel confused. I look at the dark-haired man in the doorway. He is a very good-looking man, I tell myself.

The tall man turns and I watch his eyes meet mine. I notice that he's dressed similar to the man in the portrait: a linen shirt under a black vest and he is wearing pants and boots. Although, he must be in his late twenties, I think he looks reserved and intimidating.

Matthew didn't mention a man like this living here, I thought uneasily.

The man shakes his head, and then he clears his throat.

"I'm Gerard Blackwell's niece," I say nervously.

Now I feel embarrassed for staring at him. My nervous voice made the mortification even worse. I wish I could start over and introduce myself properly, I think to myself.

The second example below is written in the Deep POV method and has lots of "voice,'" which makes it an up close-and-personal experience for the reader.

DEEP POV:

As we stand there staring at each other, a thrilling electric current courses through my body and short-circuits my brain. I blink several times at the dark-haired man standing in the doorway, trying not to stare at his eyes, an intense shade of blue. Damn, he's better looking than most of the male fashion models I've photographed.

Mr. Tall, Dark, and Yummy tilts his head and his eyes lock on mine. Even from a distance, I can tell he'll tower over me, and I'm no midget. He's even dressed similar to the man in the portrait: a soft, white linen shirt—bulging biceps stretching the fabric—under a black vest paired with snug pants and boots. Although, he appears to be only in his late twenties, he looks reserved and intimidating.

Conclusion: no sense of style, but still smoking hot.

Matthew didn't mention anyone like *him* living on the property. Having eye candy like him around will be a nice distraction. The hottie regains his composure and clears his throat.

Stop acting like a drooling idiot and speak to him!

"Hello. I'm, uh, Gerard Blackwell's niece."

My face heats. That was brilliant. Great first impression. I could really, really use a do-over so I don't come across as an ogling idiot.

***

As you revise your own work, strive to look for the simplest clarification to remove the sensory filter words from your sentences and replace those offenders with Deep POV.

CONCLUSION

Quote: "I am always chilled and astonished by the would-be writers who ask me for advice and admit, quite blithely, that they "don't have time to read." This is like a guy starting up Mount Everest saying that he didn't have time to buy any rope or pitons." —*bestselling author, Stephen King*

Now that you have a clearer idea on how to revise shallow scenes by using the Deep POV technique, try to revise your sentences by applying this amazing technique and it will take your writing skills to the next level.

And I strongly recommend that writers begin studying more books on this wonderful editing method. Although, most guidebooks will probably offer similar advice about the "show don't tell" method, writers can still gain the balance of study, theory, and practice that they might need to fully grasp and apply these wonderful skills. If you'd like to discover even more ways to strengthen your prose, I suggest studying these insightful books by these talented writers.

Recommended reading:

"Rivet Your Readers with Deep Point of View" by Jill Elizabeth Nelson

"*Mastering Showing vs. Telling in Your Fiction*" by Marcy Kennedy

"*The Emotion Thesaurus*" by Angela Ackerman and Becca Puglisi

"*The Art of Description: Bring Settings to Life*" by Anne Marble

"*How to Write Dazzling Dialogue*" by James Scott Bell

"*Take Your Pants Off*" by Libbie Hawker

***

Well, that concludes my advice on self-editing those annoying filter words and how to revise your wonderful story into Deeper POV.

Don't forget to read, "The Writer's Guide to Deep POV" (book 2), the next guidebook in this bestselling series, with even more amazing ways to hone your writing skills. And I have included a few bonus excerpts from the other guidebooks in this popular series, so please read on!

Happy revising!

S. A. Soule

HUMBLE REQUEST

If you read this handbook and find the tools and tips helpful to improving your own storytelling abilities, please consider posting an honest review on Amazon, Barnes & Noble, or Goodreads.

Word of mouth is crucial for any author's success, and reviews help to spread the book love. So please consider leaving a short (a sentence or two is fine!) review wherever you purchased this copy and/or on Goodreads.

If I get enough reviews stating that this guide helped writers to hone their craft, then I'd love to include additional books in this Deep POV series with new topics, such as romance, suspense, and world-building.

And please visit my blog, "Fiction Writing Tools," for tons of helpful advice on book promotion, author branding, and self-editing.

BONUS GUIDEBOOK TWO

THE WRITER'S GUIDE TO DEEP POV (Book 2)

Fastest Way to Improve Dialogue, Settings, and Characterization!

No matter what genre you write, this second manual on the Deep Point of View technique should be kept as a vital reference in every writer's toolbox. This in-depth guide offers specific, practical tools for creative fiction writers on how to craft realistic settings, visceral responses, and lifelike characters.

Crammed with even more examples and ways to eliminate shallow writing, this book provides the necessary techniques to master describing facial expressions, body language, and character emotions. This resource of endless inspiration will reveal how to dig deeper to "show don't tell," which is essential to crafting compelling scenes and deepening characterization.

Learn to write:

* *Realistic settings through sensory details*

* *Three-dimensional characters*

Memorable "Voice"

* *Authentic facial expressions*

Learn surefire, simple methods of getting readers so emotionally invested in your stories that booklovers will be flipping the pages to find out what happens next.

REALISTIC SETTINGS

Quote: "Don't tell me the moon is shining; show me the glint of light on the broken glass." —*playwright and short story writer, Anton Chekhov*

This chapter explains why Deep Point-of-View is one of the best editing techniques that you can use to create a realistic setting through sensory details without giving readers a weak or bland visual. The tools and tips in this section will demonstrate how writers can revise filter words used in shallower descriptions by transforming the setting into a much stronger visual.

By incorporating sensory details into a setting, along with vivid descriptions, writers can easily stay in Deeper POV. So, don't tell me that the house was on fire, instead *show* me the blaze and let me feel the heat on my skin.

Here are four simple techniques to make a setting more visual:

1) Make the landscape active by having characters interact within it.

2) Use color to add an extra depth to the scenery.

3) Make the setting a vital part of the scene.

4) Use the five senses to make the backdrop more realistic.

Sometimes writers need to simply and quickly convey details or information to the reader and move on, but if a writer applies Deeper POV on occasion, then they can bring the reader into the scene as intimately as possible.

For instance, when depicting a location/setting, describe things the way only your unique character sees them through their unique "voice" and include a few significant sensory details.

But when writers use "There was" or "There are" at the beginning of a sentence to describe an object or a setting, it creates a weak visual. These words add nothing to the scene, and sentences with these phrases can become wordy and flavorless.

Look at some examples...

WEAK: There are many witches living in the woods.

GOOD: Many witches live in the woods.

WEAK: There was a desk and a bed and lamp in the bedroom.

GOOD: The room contained an unmade bed, a dusty desk, and a tall brass lamp.

***

What usually draws a reader deeply into a story is the use of language and the way a writer describes a setting through the head and heart of their characters. One way to do that is to include a few of the five senses in every scene by describing them for the reader.

Please compare these next two examples...

SHALLOW:

There was a big table in the dining room and it looked like the wood was rotting. When I touched the surface it felt rough and dusty.

Now, the next example states the facts while giving readers enough of a visual to "see" the table in their mind's eye and experience the "touch" through sensory details without describing it in a boring way.

DEEPER POV:

A wooden table, its surface peeling away like brown bark, sat in the unused dining room. As my fingers trailed along its uneven surface, specks of dust coated my fingertips.

***

Quote: "...[if the writer] gives us such details about the streets, stores, weather, politics, and details about the looks, gestures, and experiences of his characters, we cannot help believing that the story is true." —*author "The Art of Fiction" John Gardner*

***

Showing is always much more powerful and explicit than just *telling* the reader, but it can often be more wordy. Yet I wouldn't let that hinder your use of this amazing tool. Sure, simply *telling* the reader can be a faster way to convey a lot of details about the setting, or things like a character's backstory and events; however, it is usually written in a way that is non-descript and slow and inelegant. It often creates long blocks of text without much "white space," or even "voice" within the narrative.

When readers see more than a page of thick text, they know it is straight exposition. That means no action or dialogue, which equals no forward movement of the plot. Which usually means: *boring.*

Have I made this offense? I'm sure I have, but I try very hard to avoid it.

My advice is to never push "pause" on your story to dump out long rambles of introspection or tedious facts about the setting. Although, I realize with some genres like high-fantasy or science fiction lots of world-building is needed, the descriptions can still be cleverly woven within the narrative.

Let's start with the description-dump. (In my guidebook, *The Writer's Guide to Vivid Scenes and Characters,* I provide even more examples on how to avoid doing an info-dump of description.)

When describing a room don't just catalog items or furniture like a monotonous list of inventory. To successfully create a visual scene, you need to balance the action of your characters with the description of the scene, along with the sensory details. Do not give your readers a weak visual through shallower writing.

(In the shallow example, I did not underline the obvious areas of shallower writing, but see if you can easily spot it.)

Please carefully compare these examples...

SHALLOW:

Sarah entered the room. There was a lamp, a couch, a tall grandfather clock and some letters on the table in the living room. Sarah saw some blood on the floor. She also observed a really bad smell. When she noticed the lifeless corpse, she got scared. When she heard the clock rang out the hour, she loudly screamed.

DEEP POV (sensory details):

Cautiously, Sarah tiptoed toward the dusty antique lamp and switched it on. Muted light illuminated the space. The stench of decay assaulted her senses as she weaved around the velvet sofa and past an oak table, which held a stack of unopened mail.

On the Oriental rug lay a bloody butcher's knife. Her eyes widened and her pulse thumped. Sarah backed up slowly into a towering grandfather clock. Her gaze followed the trail of blood over to a body, still and pale.

When the clock bonged midnight, she screamed.

***

Explanations of events are much more dramatic if your readers are directly involved and experiencing them along with the character. Readers may skim long pages of unbroken description; however, if it is slipped in as part of the action, then it is absorbed by the reader almost without being noticed, and enhances the scene. Always try to mix description with dialogue, actions, and the emotions of your characters.

BONUS GUIDEBOOK THREE

THE WRITER'S GUIDE TO VIVID SETTINGS AND CHARACTERS (Book 3)

Learn to Describe a Realistic Setting with Atmospheric Detail and Create Vivid Characters!

No matter what genre you write, fiction writers will learn how to craft descriptions like a seasoned pro. World-building isn't easy, but creating original depictions of characters, locations, weather, and mood can greatly enhance anyone's writing.

Evocative settings are more effective and compelling when they're visible, auditory, olfactory, and tactile. And character descriptions are much more visual and lifelike when they have unique physical attributes. This valuable reference and descriptive thesaurus offers writers a simplified way to depict vibrant settings and dynamic character descriptions flawlessly.

Writers will learn:

* The importance of using sensory details

* To expertly master showing vs. telling

* The impact setting can have on a story

* To effectively describe vivid characters

* How adding color will strengthen description

Each chapter provides specific, practical tools to help make writing descriptions and crafting three-dimensional characters simple and fun, with plenty of illustrations to highlight each point.

WRITING DESCRIPTION

Quote: "Try to cut down on your adjectives and adverbs. Modifiers don't specify words as much as you might think. More often than not, they actually abstract a thought, so sentences that rely on modifiers for descriptive strength are building on faulty foundations. You'll be more successful if you instead find the verb that perfectly portrays the image you're envisioning. When you edit your work, spend considerable time scrutinizing your sentences to make sure the action maximizes full descriptive potential." —*editor and writer, Jon Gingerich*

If you've finished writing a novel or short story, then congratulations! That is a huge accomplishment to be very proud of, but now comes the revision work that will *really* make your story shine…

This book should help writers create dramatic scenes and illustrate how to craft a distinct and realistic world filled with three-dimensional characters, vivid locations, and naturalistic weather. Throughout this guide, writers will learn how they can use the five senses to arouse the reader's own senses of sight, touch, hear, smell, taste, and even feel. I'll even illustrate ways a writer of any genre can revise boring description info-dumps into a mood that harmonizes nicely with the novel's storyline, and how to craft unique descriptions of characters, locations, and climate.

Each chapter provides specific, practical tools to help make writing descriptions and crafting lifelike characters simple and fun, with plenty of examples to highlight each point.

The writing tools provided in this book cover many topics, such as:

* The importance of using sensory details

* How nouns and verbs impact description

* A thesaurus of descriptive words

* How to revise description info-dumps of places and characters

* How to expertly master showing vs. telling

* The impact setting can have on a story

* How to effectively describe life-like characters

* How adding color will strengthen descriptions

* How using the weather can create mood and atmosphere

* How the five senses can enhance the narrative

* How nature can enrich the background

Any fiction writer who has taken a creative writing course, received a professional edit on their manuscript, or worked with a critique partner has undoubtedly heard these three words: *show, don't tell.*

In my opinion, fiction is mostly about establishing a visceral, emotional connection between the character(s) and the reader. One way to do this is by *showing* instead of *telling.* Writers can use the Deep POV method to *show,* which creates vibrant and dramatic images within the reader's mind that will deeply immerse them in any fictional world.

Personally, I love writing descriptions of settings and characters, but as a freelance fiction editor, the majority of writers that I've worked with forget to include any details regarding the setting or their characters. While I'm reading and critiquing their work, I'm not connecting to the story if I can't envision the setting (where the story unfolds or where a scene happens) or even the characters themselves.

Description isn't optional in fiction. Every scene should include some details pertaining to the environment. It's imperative to effective world-building. If writers can make the settings original and colorful, the description will infuse your fictional world with mood and atmosphere.

For instance, if a new scene starts with two characters talking, but there's no mention of where the scene takes place or where the characters are, then it leaves me with a weak visual. Writers don't need to go into too much detail, but some is helpful in order to cement the scene and keep the characters from seeming as though they're floating around in space instead of being firmly anchored to the fictional world where they exist.

In the early drafts of a manuscript, *telling* is expected. It's more important to get the story finished and the plot holes filled in, then to worry about if a writer is *showing* enough. It's during the revision stage of later drafts (more like draft five or six) when it's time to polish the settings, include character descriptions, and check for red flags of *telling* throughout the narrative.

Writers should want readers to experience the story through the senses of their characters. And by engaging the five senses, it helps readers connect more closely with the character's experience. Shallow sentences with filter words will have the opposite effect.

Please compare these descriptive examples...

SHALLOW: I touched the dress to feel the fabric.

SHOWING: My fingers caressed the silky fabric.

If you're going to describe how something tastes, sounds and looks, then you can leave out how it feels and smells. You never want to assault your reader's senses, or they will skip ahead to get back to the action.

Please compare the next two examples...

SHALLOW: When Scott heard the growling sound, he looked down and saw a large dog blocking the trail. He knew it would attack if he moved. Scott felt a sense of terror build in his heart.

SHOWING: Scott halted at the warning growl. Standing in front of him was a large dog, flashing its teeth. He stifled the girlish shriek that leaked from his lips with one hand. Scott took a stumbling step backward, his heart jackhammering in his chest.

***

In the second example, you can imagine much more easily the dog and Scott's emotional response. It's always better to attempt to make your scene unique by inserting some of the five senses into the narrative.

To encourage fiction writers to craft stunning scenes, vivid characters, and lush settings, I have included references from my own personal database of descriptions in this guidebook. And I have created lots of examples to demonstrate how writers can avoid narrative distance in easy to grasp methods that can instantly improve anyone's writing.

Throughout this guide, I'll be discussing how writers can enhance elements of a story in any genre by incorporating a description of the locations, landscapes, and characters in each scene, with several simple techniques for creating sensory details to enhance the world-building.

BONUS GUIDEBOOK FOUR

THE WRITER'S GUIDE TO AUTHENTIC DIALOGUE

A Powerful Reference Tool to Crafting Realistic Conversations in Fiction!

This manual is specifically for fiction writers who want to learn how to create riveting and compelling dialogue that propels the storyline and reveals character personality.

Writers will also learn how to weave emotion, description, and action into their dialogue heavy scenes. With a special section on how to instantly improve characterization through gripping conversations. All of these helpful writing tools will make your dialogue sparkle!

DIALOGUE TAGS

Quote: "Writing convincing dialogue is one of the hardest things for new writers to master. In fact, it's so rarely done well in any form of fiction that when it is done right, people rally around it. The movie Pulp Fiction, Terry McMillan's novel Waiting to Exhale, and the TV series My So-Called Life were all remarkable in large part because of how believably the characters spoke." —*Science Fiction writer, Robert J. Sawyer*

This first chapter covers basics such as how to use dialogue tags or beats correctly. As a professional developmental editor, I critique hundreds of manuscripts for fiction writers and dialogue seems the hardest for writers to write well. Personally, I use a software program that reads the text out loud for me. It's great to hear the rhythm and flow of your character interactions and the conversations to make sure the dialogue sounds natural. If you don't have access to a program, which can read your text for you—read it out loud to yourself. Or better yet, find someone to read it to you. It makes a *huge* difference in your dialogue.

Some of you might be wondering what the term "dialogue tag" means...

Well, "dialogue tags" are the additions to dialogue that identify the speaker. Without them, the reader would get confused as the conversations unfold, or if you have more than two characters speaking to each other within a scene. Readers need dialogue tags and saidisms that don't distract from the narrative. (Saidisms are just alternative words that mean "said" that are used to indicate additional information that is not expressed through the actual dialog or in the character description.)

Dialogue tags (also called by some writers and editors as saidisms or speech tags) are simple indications that allow the reader to identify each speaker. If there are only two characters in a scene, then it is not necessary to place a tag after each line of dialogue. Occasionally, you can use the character's unique speech patterns to distinguish which character is speaking.

Current writing style guidelines prefer that all dialogue tags identify the character first, and then the speech tag. It should be written as: "Nick said" instead of "said Nick." If you are self-publishing your work, these are the type of important writing techniques that you should keep in mind.

A good editing tool to remember is to avoid the overuse of adverbs that end in "ly." For example, "Max said mysteriously," or "Ashley said dryly" in the dialogue. Sure, a few are okay, but I suggest that writers try not to overdo it. These types of adverbs added onto the speech tags *tell* and don't *show*, which take a writer out of Deeper POV. Try to stick to using the general, "said / say" tags. The reader's eyes will simply pass over "said" and never even realize they've read it.

While acceptable, words such as "hollered" and "bawled" and "cried" often draw their attention away from the dialogue and yank your reader out of the story. So, in short, avoid saturating your dialogue scenes with tags such as: *cried, whispered, screeched, whined, declared, questioned, demanded, roared, hissed,* or *breathed.* These words appear as if you have become a little too chummy with your thesaurus. If the dialogue is well written, a few carefully placed tags like, "said/say" will often do just fine.

Also, try to avoid using too many descriptors like "yelled," or "said angrily," or "cried out," as a description of the character's emotion. The dialogue tag should allow the reader to interpret how something is being spoken without "telling" them. And remember that the word "said" is invisible to readers in dialogue text, while too many description tags can be off-putting to the reader.

While readers tend to read over the basic "said/say" tag, discernible attempts to insert a mixture of words such as "exclaimed," "shouted," or "teased," will completely pull the reader out of the narrative. If the writer has written skillful dialogue, then the reader is conscious that the character is exclaiming, bellowing, or mocking. The writer won't have to include it in the saidism.

How to write dialogue correctly:

Dialogue is set apart or identified with quotation marks. "Words spoken." To create realistic dialogue, it does not have to be written in complete sentences. In real life conversations, people don't always use proper grammar, either. So make certain that your dialogue sounds like what a person would actually say in a real conversation.

Each character needs their own individual voice.

Please make sure that all of your characters sound differently. They should not speak the same way or sound the same.

If you're writing a crime-drama, your vengeful, homicidal housewife should not sound the same as an alcoholic surgeon who just lost a patient on the operating table. Study current slang and modern trends. Give each character their own unique voice.

FICTION WRITING TOOLS

Each of these helpful and inexpensive self-editing books in the *Fiction Writing Tools* series encompass many different topics such as, dialogue, exposition, internal-monologue, setting, and other editing techniques that will help creative writers take their writing skills to the next level.

In every guide, bestselling author, S. A. Soule also shares her expertise with writers on how to apply "showing" methods through powerful examples in action, along with the necessary tools to immediately deepen the reader's experience with vivid, sensory details.

THE WRITER'S GUIDE TO DEEP POINT-OF-VIEW

Fastest Way to Improve Dialogue, Settings, and Characterization!

No matter what genre you write, this second manual on the Deep Point of View technique should be kept as a vital reference in every writer's toolbox. This in-depth guide offers specific, practical tools for creative fiction writers on how to craft realistic settings, visceral responses, and lifelike characters.

Crammed with even more examples and ways to eliminate shallow writing, this book provides the necessary techniques to master describing facial expressions, body language, and character emotions. This resource of endless inspiration will reveal how to dig deeper to "show don't tell," which is essential to crafting compelling scenes and deepening characterization.

Learn to write:

* Realistic settings through sensory details

* Three-dimensional characters

* Memorable "Voice"

*Authentic facial expressions

Learn surefire, simple methods of getting readers so emotionally invested in your stories that booklovers will be flipping the pages to find out what happens next.

THE WRITER'S GUIDE TO VIVID SETTINGS AND CHARACTERS

Learn to Describe a Realistic Setting with Atmospheric Detail and Create Vivid Characters!

No matter what genre you write, fiction writers will learn how to craft descriptions like a seasoned pro. World-building isn't easy, but creating original depictions of characters, locations, weather, and mood can greatly enhance anyone's writing.

Evocative settings are more effective and compelling when they're visible, auditory, olfactory, and tactile. And character descriptions are much more visual and lifelike when they have unique physical attributes. This valuable reference and descriptive thesaurus offers writers a simplified way to depict vibrant settings and dynamic character descriptions flawlessly.

Writers will learn:

* The importance of using sensory details

* To expertly master showing vs. telling

* The impact setting can have on a story

* To effectively describe vivid characters

* How adding color will strengthen description

Each chapter provides specific, practical tools to help make writing descriptions and crafting three-dimensional characters simple and fun, with plenty of illustrations to highlight each point.

THE WRITER'S GUIDE TO AUTHENTIC DIALOGUE

A Powerful Reference Tool to Crafting Realistic Conversations in Fiction!

This manual is specifically for fiction writers who want to learn how to create riveting and compelling dialogue that propels the storyline and reveals character personality.

Writers will also learn how to weave emotion, description, and action into their dialogue heavy scenes. With a special section on how to instantly improve characterization through gripping conversations. All of these helpful writing tools will make your dialogue sparkle!

THE WRITER'S GUIDE TO A BESTSELLING NOVEL

Awesome Tips on Crafting a Riveting Story that instantly Grabs Your Reader...

This manual offers amazing techniques for creating stronger beginnings and ways to write a page-turning plot for your fiction novel. Writers will learn how to make their first pages so intriguing with chapter "hooks" that the reader won't be able to put the book down.

Easy to follow step-by-step instructions on creating a comprehensive plot with the three-act structure using the dynamic templates provided in this guidebook, whether you're a plotter or more of a pantser. Each chapter provides comprehensive tips on storytelling, which every writer needs to plot like an experienced pro without a complicated outline.

Topics in this book include:

* 6 Popular Genre Plot Templates

* 3 Extensive Character Templates

* Tools to Create a Page-Turning First Chapter

* Advice on Writing Scene Hooks

* Simple Breakdown on Story Structure

* Wisdom from Bestselling Authors on Plotting

Also, writers will gain the tools needed to blend character goals within any scene to improve pacing, and instantly strengthen the narrative. Plus, bonus advice on self-publishing and genre word counts. Whether you're writing an intense thriller or a sweeping romance, all novels follow the same basic outline described in detail within this book.

THE WRITER'S GUIDE TO BOOK BLURBS and QUERY LETTERS

An Awesome Book Description is one of the Most Important Tools a Writer Needs to Sell More Books, or to Gain the Attention of an Agent...

Whether you're self-publishing, or querying agents and publishers, this guidebook on book descriptions can help! Writing backjacket copy (blurb or marketing copy) can give most writers a major headache. In this in-depth reference manual, any writer can learn how to instantly create an appealing blurb with a captivating tagline, or write a perfect query letter.

Indie Authors will get a clearer understanding on how to write an effective book description, which is one of the most vital selling points a self-published author needs to successfully promote a book. Book blurbs are a critical marketing tool to attract readers. (Besides a "genre specific" book cover.)

Topics in this book include:

* Book Descriptions: Each chapter offers simple steps to creating powerful blurbs with a gripping opening line, and a strong last sentence "hook."

* Blurb templates: Writers will get 4 simple blurb breakdown templates to learn how to easily write compelling marketing copy.

*Query Letters: If you're a writer, seeking an agent, then crafting an enticing query letter is crucial on the path toward traditional publication. Great cover letters are essential to attracting agents and book publishers.

* Blurb Examples: Over 25 enticing blurbs in almost every genre to unlock your own creativity for self-published novelists.

* Query Templates: Over 10 query letter templates to use for inspiration and guidance for writers striving to get a book publishing contract.

In this valuable resource, there are numerous query letters templates and book blurb examples for almost every fiction genre that will have an agent asking for more, and help a self-published author to write a compelling product description that will boost their book sales.

THE WRITER'S GUIDE TO BOOK PROMOTION

Learn How To Sell More Books in a Month!

This in-depth marketing guide is perfect for writers publishing their first novel or indie authors trying to gain a wider readership. The manual includes valuable tips on networking, how to get more book reviews, and contains wonderful advice on how to best promote your work from established authors and popular book bloggers.

Whether you're a multi-published author looking to expand your audience or a self-published writer, this book will instantly give you the tools to market your fiction like a pro! Free bonus features include how successful authors use social media to connect with potential readers, reviewers, and how to sell more books.

THESE BOOKS ARE ON SALE NOW AT ALL MAJOR ONLINE RETAILERS

BONUS MARKETING TIPS

Read on for a two more chapters filled with amazing tips on book promotion taken from my insightful guidebook, **THE WRITER'S GUIDE TO BOOK PROMOTION**, which can double your sales within six to eight weeks!

This in-depth marketing guide is perfect for writers publishing their first novel or indie authors trying to gain a wider readership. The manual includes valuable tips on networking, how to get more book reviews, and contains wonderful advice on how to best promote your work from established authors and popular book bloggers.

Whether you're a multi-published author looking to expand your audience or a self-published writer, this book will instantly give you the tools to market your fiction like a pro! Free bonus features include how successful authors use social media to connect with potential readers, reviewers, and how to sell more books.

BOOK COVERS DON'T MATTER

From the title of this chapter, you'll assume that it's the story within the novel that *really* counts and not the book cover. But that kind of thinking might hinder your sales. Now let me explain why...

If your book cover doesn't match the genre, then the story won't reach your intended audience. If the book cover isn't genre specific enough, you won't sell as many books.

I understand how difficult it can be to promote your novel(s) and generate sales, and sometimes a writer can't afford a cover designer. Or it just isn't high on a writer's list of priorities. Or maybe they thought the book cover doesn't matter that much and a cover won't help with sales.

BUT a cover is usually what first attracts the reader and lures them in. A book cover is the first impression that most readers have. It is like bait on a hook that captures the reader's attention and gets them curious enough to want to find out more.

A good cover is part of a writer's marketing arsenal and it had better do a damn good job!

Potential readers are searching for novels that have these six elements:

Resembles the genre they read

Has a familiar / similar look as other books in the genre

Have characters with intriguing problems

Reminds them of other books they've read and enjoyed

Has an interesting concept or blurb

A cover that instantly snags the reader's attention

Having a DYI (do-it-yourself) cover (if you don't know anything about designing a book cover) or an amateurish looking design will kill your book sales faster than anything else, no matter how awesome and compelling and unique the writing is, if the book cover doesn't reflect the genre.

***

Quote: "COVERS ARE STOP SIGNS. They should quickly reveal as much info about your book to the reader as possible and this did not. As soon as I changed the covers to the current version, sales shot up ... Short version: I was really stupid. Don't wait nine months to change covers or descriptions on books that aren't preforming." -H. M. Ward is a *New York Times* bestselling indie author, with millions of books sold.

***

Personally, I also made a lot of mistakes in cover art when I was first starting out in the indie publishing world, so please take this advice to heart!

For example, even though I told the designers that I hired exactly what I wanted for a book cover, I didn't bother checking to see what other covers in my genre resembled or study the market. I just told them to create something I thought was cool. Really stupid of me...

Although, I still like my previous covers, I now realize that the fonts weren't right for the genre, nor the background images, or color schemes. So, I studied the market (checked out my competition) and took a long hard look at what covers were trending in the genre that I was writing...

My book sales have tripled shortly after I redid my covers and made them more genre specific. I finally did something smart, and I went with a cover that reflected the genre and hit my target audience.

My advice is to have a cover that is genre specific. Put some cash aside and get yourself a book cover designed, or even buy a premade in your genre that reflects what's on the bestseller's lists. And it is NOT copying or generic to have a cover that gives readers instant recognition of the story and genre.

Again, that is the covers only main job.

Hope this advice helps boost your sales!

Please don't forget to visit **SwoonWorthy Book Covers** to browse a huge selection of inexpensive premade book cover designs in almost every genre!

TIPS ON BOOK COVER DESIGN

Over the years, I've definitely made my fair share of mistakes as a self-published writer and indie author. Although, I'd hired talented book cover designers, I didn't bother to do any research. I just told the designer what I wanted without spending anytime studying the market, or other books in my genre. I should've checked the bestseller lists and taken a closer look at my competition. My book covers were amazing, but they didn't quite fit the trends in design at that time.

For example, I write young adult novels in both the paranormal romance and science fiction genres. When those novels were first published, I didn't take the time do any marketing research. *Big mistake!* My books just weren't selling as much I'd hoped until I changed my covers to designs that better matched the genres trending, and within six weeks my sales tripled.

It is smart to have a cover that matches the genre and follows the trends of other book covers.

Lately, I've noticed a lot of really ugly, amateurish looking book covers that were clearly DIY. (*Sometimes I really want to contact these authors and offer them a free design, but I'm afraid that would be rude!*) That's one reason why I decided to start creating inexpensive book covers for indie authors on a budget. Nowadays, self-published authors must wear many hats, like becoming a marketing expert.

A book cover (packaging) is important.

A lot of writers think the book cover design doesn't matter, but it does have a huge impact on reaching the right readership and expressing the genre.

If your book isn't selling and you've been promoting it for months and the reviews are decent, but sales are still dragging, then it might be time to replace your cover. Even with something standard that resembles the genre that you write. Or if you're not sure if your book cover fits your genre, I suggest studying the design trends on the bestsellers lists and visit goodreads and browse through the book covers in whichever genre and sub-genres that you write in.

Some articles online I recently found were actually shaming book cover designs that were too similar. These blog posts are misleading to indie authors based on an incorrect assumption that covers need to be completely original and unpredictable.

A book cover just needs to look professional, with fonts and colors that match the general design standards for that genre, and let readers immediately know the basic category of the novel. A successful book cover should also be similar to other bestsellers in the same genre. It is that simple.

I wish everyone much success in their writing career!

ABOUT THE AUTHOR

S. A. Soule is a bestselling author and Creativity Coach, who has years of experience working with successful novelists. Many of her fiction and non-fiction books have spent time on the bestseller lists.

Her handbooks in the "Fiction Writing Tools" series are a great resource for writers at any stage in their career, and they each offer helpful tips on how to instantly take your writing skills to the next level and successfully promote your books.

Please feel free to browse her blog, which has some great tips on creative writing online at: *Fiction Writing Tools* and visit her *Creativity Coaching Services* site for help with writing book blurbs, fiction editing, and revising stories with Deep POV.

Made in the USA
Columbia, SC
16 October 2018